EXPERTS HAIL
WORKING WOUNDED™

"WORKING WOUNDED is right on the money, delivering smart advice that makes you smile."
> —JANE BRYANT QUINN, *Newsweek* columnist and author of *Making the Most of Your Money*

"I've known Bob Rosner to be full of opinion and attitude since I recruited him to write a monthly sports column for our high school newspaper. Now he has written a book on how you can survive the workplace with dignity and, well, attitude. Bob's book is salve for the working stiff."
> —JEFFREY L. SEGLIN, executive editor of *Inc. Magazine*

"A lively treatment of a sore subject . . . an ample mix of wisdom, humor, and empathy."
> —WILLIAM D. RUCKELSHAUS, chairman of Browning-Ferris Industries and founding director of the Environmental Protection Agency

"WORKING WOUNDED is not only a friend of the working person, it also offers skills and tools to survive in the workplace. If you're employed, you need to read it."
> —WALLY AMOS, author of *Watermelon Magic: Seeds of Wisdom, Slices of Life*

more . . .

"Funny . . . helpful . . . balm for the 'working wounded' across America. His advice on becoming an entrepreneur is right on target."

> —JANE APPLEGATE, syndicated small business columnist and author of *201 Great Ideas for Your Small Business*

"Readers will learn something new and will certainly enjoy this book."

> —HANS GUTSCH, senior vice president of human resources and environment for Compaq Computer Corporation

"We are all, at one time or another, one of the 'working wounded.' This is a fabulous compilation of some of the best business advice about coping in the workplace."

> —JULIE BICK, author of *All I Really Need to Know in Business I Learned at Microsoft*

WORKING WOUNDED™

Advice that Adds Insight to Injury

BOB ROSNER

WARNER BOOKS

A Time Warner Company

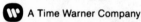
Printed in the United States of America
First Printing: March 1998
10 9 8 7 6 5 4 3 2 1

Library of Congress Cataloging-in-Publication Data

Rosner, Bob.
    Working wounded : advice that adds insight to injury / Bob Rosner.
        p. cm.
    "Working wounded . . . a syndicated business advice column with an
affiliated TV news segment and web site . . .
(http://workingwounded.com)"—P. 4.
    ISBN 0-446-52289-9
    1. Office politics. 2. Office politics—Humor. 3. Corporate
culture. 4. Corporate culture—Humor. 5. Success in business.
6. Success in business—Humor.   I. Title.
HF5386.5.R67 1998
651.1'3—dc21   97-27159
                                                              CIP

Book design and composition by L&G McRee

To learn more about this book and author, visit
http://workingwounded.com

Dedicated to everyone who's been wounded at work.
(But remember, in the words of Kafka,
"We too have weapons.")

IS THIS BOOK FOR YOU?

1. How do you feel about your job?

  a. It's like walking up the down escalator
  b. It's like a concrete overcoat
  c. It's like underwear that's too tight
  d. It's like an old pair of jeans

2. By and large my co-workers . . .

  a. Are more interested in my business than doing theirs
  b. Can push my buttons better than my parents
  c. Co-workers? You mean the people over there playing computer solitaire?
  d. Are people I trust and enjoy

3. How secure do you feel in your job?

  a. Like I'm living on borrowed time
  b. I'll never get out of here, it's like quicksand
  c. Like a neighborhood mom-and-pop store going up against Wal-Mart
  d. I've already picked out my gold watch

4. Do a good job in my company and you get . . .

  a. A pat on the back
  b. Are you kidding? Only the muckety-mucks get credit for anything around here

c. In my company there is no such thing as a job well done

d. The three Rs: respect, recognition and rewards

5. Does work seem to be rigged in "their" favor?

a. Yeah, it's rigged by my boss

b. Yeah, it's rigged by my competitors

c. Yeah, it's rigged by a clique of my co-workers

d. Nah, it feels pretty fair to me

6. If they made a movie about your company, who would play your boss?

a. Darth Vader

b. Kramer

c. Scrooge

d. Glinda, the good witch

Give yourself 1 point for every a, b or c answer and 2 points for every d answer.

If you scored:

6 or less You're one of the working wounded. Find a comfortable chair because you've got a lot of reading to do.

7 to 11 You're in the target zone. Keep reading for tips on how to dodge the bullets.

12 Is your company hiring? Whom should I send my résumé to?

CONTENTS

Contents

WHAT BUGS YOU ABOUT WORK?

- **Everything?** See Chapter 1, *Shot Full of Holes,* for the Working Wounded approach to work and philosophy.
- **Your co-workers?** See Chapter 2, *Poked from All Sides,* for tips on protecting yourself from tripping over their baggage.
- **Your boss?** See Chapter 3, *Pummeled from Above,* for tips on getting the autonomy and recognition you deserve.
- **Your employees?** See Chapter 4, *Battered from Below,* for pointers on managing against the odds.
- **Missing a promotion?** See Chapter 5, *Squeezed into a Box,* to learn Career Monopoly, the game that can advance your career.
- **Getting out?** See Chapter 6, *Struggling to Get Out,* for tips on breaking out of your current job and into one that's better.
- **Making the sale?** See Chapter 7, *Pushed to Perform,* to make sales (and salespeople) less deadly.
- **Stress?** See Chapter 8, *Staying Alive,* for tips on punching back when the clock punches you.
- **Dealing with new technology?** See Chapter 9, *Stuck in the Web,* for tips on making technology your partner.

- **Feeling like you're about to be let go?** See Chapter 10, *Shoved out the Door,* for tips on toughening your exit and softening your landing.
- **Dreams of being on your own?** See Chapter 11, *Sick and Tired and Ready to Be My Own Boss,* for tips on making it as an entrepreneur.
- **Wondering what it all means?** See Chapter 12, *Dodging the Bullets,* for tips on finding satisfaction on the job.

When I walk on stage, I've got to feel like it's the most important thing in the world. Also I got to feel like, well, it's only rock and roll.

BRUCE SPRINGSTEEN, still my favorite "Boss"

CHAPTER 1

SHOT FULL OF HOLES

Just Trying to Survive 9 to 5

ARE YOU ONE OF THE WORKING WOUNDED?

Have you taken a few bullets in the course of your career? I'm not talking about disgruntled postal workers here; I'm talking about the other kind of workplace "bullet" that can wound your heart, your mind and your career. You know the ammo: inflexible bosses, irritating co-workers, counterproductive corporate policies and the like. Well, over the years I've met plenty of people who were wounded on the job, but scar for scar none can match Jane—and what she taught me about workplace survival.

1

I'd been hired as a consultant to help restructure a large department at an insurance company, and since tensions had mounted during the project I'd invited several of the key players to my home for a purely social evening. We were well into dinner before the conversation drifted away from shoptalk, but as I got up to pass the pasta for the second time I heard Jane, a manager in the department, talking about her sinuses.

"That's why I'm out so much," she was saying. "I've had trouble with my sinuses ever since I was shot."

"Ever since you were *what?*"

"Ever since I was shot."

Instantly, a dozen voices broke out. "You were shot!" "When were you shot?" "Who shot you?"

Jane shrugged as if it were the most natural thing in the world. "Oh, my ex-husband shot me, but luckily the bullet lodged in my head." She pointed to the left of her nose. "I've had a devil of a sinus problem ever since."

Instantly the room grew still. I could guess what people were thinking. Jane had taken a lot of flak for her frequent absences. People begrudged her the time away and resented picking up her slack. A few had even tried to bar her from a key committee as a form of retaliation. Now, in light of her revelation, they were feeling guilty about their behavior.

Jane laughed as she described the challenges of

going through airport security machines and getting X rays from unsuspecting doctors ("I don't know how to break this to you, ma'am, but you seem to have a bullet in your head"). And as she talked, words of support and consolation spread around the table. By the time we adjourned at close to midnight, the co-workers were more congenial than I'd ever seen them. The dinner didn't resolve the tension created by the department's restructuring, but it did go a long way toward smoothing relations between Jane and her colleagues.

Well, Jane is the only person I've ever met who actually had a bullet in her head. But I've met plenty of others who *felt* as if they had one—or who wanted to put one into someone else's. Because that's the nature of the workplace: one person's actions, whether intentional or unintended, can send shrapnel flying through the organization.

"Oh, fine. And you?" "Never better."

MAYBE THEY SHOULD CALL IT
UNFRIENDLY FIRE

I bet you've even taken some ammo yourself. Ever felt like you were pummeled into submission by an unfair boss? Or like you were poked till it hurt by cantankerous co-workers? Or like you were being squeezed by a system that wasn't giving you adequate recognition? If so, welcome to the working wounded—you've taken your share of workplace flak.

And you don't need to be a line worker to be in the line of fire. Bosses get wounded, too; so do entrepreneurs. Perhaps you've felt battered by customers who thought that therapy was included in the warranty. Or by employees whose specialty was pushing your buttons. Or by bankers who wanted proof that your business didn't need a loan before they'd deign to approve one. Whatever your position, shots to the head, heart and wallet are unavoidable at work—even in a job you love.

The irony, of course, is that most of us could handle the flak if it just came from our competitors. But it doesn't. Most of it comes from people who are supposed to be on our side. Or worse still, it's self-inflicted—due to miscommunication, or to good intentions gone astray, or just to our own thickheadedness.

ADVICE THAT ADDS INSIGHT TO INJURY

That's why I created Working Wounded™. I'd been a consultant to the Fortune 500 and the U.S. government, gotten an MBA and taught in an MBA program, and founded three corporations (one for-profit and two nonprofits). In short, I'd had a lot of contact with a lot of people in a lot of different settings. And I'd begun to realize that the one thing that could keep people in the workplace even later at night than the race to make an artificial deadline was the chance to *talk* about the race to make an artificial deadline. People need to talk about their jobs! But ironically, while there were radio shows, advice columns and Web sites on virtually every other aspect of human endeavor—from nurturing relationships to fixing carburetors to growing zucchini—there was no public forum in which people could come together to laugh and learn about their jobs. Except for Dilbert—that font of workplace wit and wisdom—there wasn't anything that spoke to ordinary people about what *really* goes on at work. And there was nothing that gave people customized, practical information for tackling their work and career dilemmas. To paraphrase Lily Tomlin, together we were all going through work alone.

So I created Working Wounded—the anti-guru guru (or, as one of my first editors called it, "the Martha Stewart of the underemployed"). It's a syndicated business advice column (with an affiliated TV news segment and Web site) that doesn't taste like medicine and that doesn't pretend that the solutions to all workplace problems involve reengineering, TQM, teamwork or anything with "one minute" in the title. On the contrary, Working Wounded believes that the solutions to your workplace problems must be devised and implemented by *you*. (After all, they're your problems so who else could possibly fix them?)

Of course, I'm not there with you in the trenches, dealing with your boss, your boss's boss, your nemesis in another department or your idiosyncratic corporate culture. So I can't tell you exactly what to do. But I've found that telling people what to do rarely works, anyway. So instead I ask a lot of questions to help you analyze your situation. Then I offer strategies that have been proven in the real world to mitigate that kind of problem. Finally, I give you another place to turn if you'd like more information.

The advice in Working Wounded comes from a world that is normally off limits to all but the corner-office in crowd. For instance, we take our readers' questions to $350 an hour attorneys (the same ones who normally represent the company), to directors of human resources, a.k.a. personnel (who reveal the resources they use to manage worker complaints), and to specialists in a variety of workplace issues. These folks give readers the same advice they usually give to corporations after the companies have paid really big bucks. So in a way, Working Wounded is like an HR department for the rest of us. All expenses paid.

And because Working Wounded is an award-winning site on the World Wide Web (*http://workingwounded.com*) we also have our ear to the people's grapevine. That means we can gather feedback from all over the world about how to handle similar problems, and we can provide polls and surveys as well as people's own strategies for addressing the issues covered in the book.

How did I decide what issues to cover in this book? It's simple: I let our readers decide. Cranky co-workers, ballistic bosses, how to deal with technology, how to get out . . . those are the issues readers write to us about, so those are the issues we've included. I answer the most universal letters, the ones that have the broadest appeal, so that, hopefully, all readers will get something out of the columns. Here I've arranged them by subject category—so you can quickly find exactly the information you need to scratch your particular itch.

BUT I'M NOT WOUNDED

And what if you're not having problems? Why bother reading this book? Because you never know what to expect . . . as I learned from experience.

Back in college I took a course in abnormal psychology. (No, I wasn't the subject of the class.)

One day the professor lectured on the behavioral psychologist B. F. Skinner, and as he described an experiment in which Skinner trained pigeons to spot defects in a product with nearly 100 percent accuracy, the woman next to me began to cry. I knew it was impolite, but I had to ask what was making her cry. "I just got fired from my job," she sniffed. "I'm sorry," I whispered. "Don't be sorry," she sobbed. "I hated the job. But I worked in quality control. *I'm not even as good as a pigeon!*"

Well, that day I learned there's not much you can say to a woman who just lost her job to a bird. I also learned that work is full of the unexpected. You never know what's going to fly in from left field, or where the stuff is going to land. So you've got to be prepared. And that's where Working Wounded can help. We can't prevent your getting sacked by a pigeon, but we *can* help you protect yourself from a lot of the flying debris.

And that brings me back to Jane. Despite her bullet, her sinus condition and the flak she took from colleagues—Jane never thought of herself as a victim. She came early and stayed late almost daily to minimize the burden on her co-workers. She thwarted her colleagues' efforts to keep her off the committee by presenting a well-documented case to her supervisor. And she managed, through it all, to maintain a largely positive outlook—as if, having survived a real bullet, from a lethally abusive ex-spouse, she was not about to be flattened by the ones that were fired at work. And in that respect, Jane exemplified the Working Wounded philosophy: she knew that friendly fire is inescapable, but that it's sometimes possible to minimize the damage.

Fortunately *you* don't need to survive live ammo to minimize your damage. You only need to read this book. Because Working Wounded isn't about whining over your wounds; it's about what you can do to rise above them. Think of it as your personal Kevlar vest. It gives you the "ahah's" and the "haha's" you need to deflect those bullets at work.

"Davis, come in here and take a bullet."

from email to *workingwounded.com*

After They've Eaten Away at Your Trust—Bite Back!

The worst co-worker in the world has got to be the one you can't trust—and we have one like that at our office. Problem is, we're not sure who it is! But almost every day, someone's lunch disappears from the office fridge. Worse yet, the thief often eats PART of the selected lunch and leaves the rest. For example, one time he or she ate just the meatballs from somebody's homemade spaghetti. Another time, the thief ate four pieces of someone's fried chicken, threw the bones back in the box and sealed it up. But we've got a plan. We're going to install a hidden video camera in the break room and catch the thief red-handed. Then we're going to make him take us all out to lunch at the most expensive restaurant in town!

from email to *workingwounded.com*

Johnny Paycheck Would Be Proud

I was fired mid-shift from my bartending job by my drunk manager. I walked from the bar, disgruntled but calm, and with the encouragement and help of most of the patrons managed to play "Take This Job and Shove It" thirty-two times (it took the numbskull that long to figure out he could unplug the machine). What a way to go.

The Working Wounded Quotebook

" "

Things do not change, we change.

THOREAU

CHAPTER 2

POKED FROM ALL SIDES
How to Cope with Your Co-Workers

WHAT'S THAT YOU'RE CARRYING?

Do you sometimes feel like your co-workers are an occupational hazard? If so, the following story may give you a new perspective on those "idiosyncratic" folks you work with. Maybe, even, on yourself.

I hadn't seen Jim in ten years, since high school. As we guzzled our beers we caught up on jobs, high school buddies, our favorite sports team; gradually we got to the subject of girlfriends. To our surprise, we were both dating women in their thirties, five or six years older than we were, and we began to muse about our attraction to older women. They had more insight and experience we agreed, and just plain more to say.

More beers passed and we moved to the downside of older girlfriends. On this we also agreed: they carried more baggage—emotional scars from former boyfriends, eagerness to get married, readiness to have kids—and all that baggage made them a little tough to handle. We commiserated over the challenges: Jim's girlfriend felt he wasn't "serious" enough about life (though he felt *seriously* committed to the Yankees, his record collection and Chinese takeout). Mine was ready to pick out china (as ready as I was to blow my job, hop in a car and head across the country). We shared these little truths, sipped our beers and laughed, and then, as we mused on what we'd said, another shocking truth came clear: *we had baggage, too!* These little "preferences," these harmless quirks that made us who we were, were just as loaded as anything our girlfriends brought! We paid our bill and ambled out into the night, a little drunk and more than a little chastened.

Of course the baggage didn't stop accumulating just because we'd noticed it. In the ensuing years it continued to pile up, bruising the shins of girlfriends, friends and parents. And because we didn't leave it behind when we headed off to work each morning, we raised bruises on some of our co-workers, too. Nothing major, mind you. Just the usual sores and irritations that erupt when your personal baggage colors your relationships with colleagues.

That's what makes the workplace so darned treacherous. *We all have baggage. And we're constantly tripping over each other's stuff.* You know how it works: you do your part of a project only to have a team member miss the deadline, passive aggression leaking from his crankcase like old 10/40 oil. You support a colleague's idea only to engender another colleague's wrath: turns out she's a walking bundle of insecurity and she feels threatened. There's so much emotional baggage strewn around the workplace there's *no way* to navigate without sustaining bruises. In fact, most of the time I wonder how anything gets done.

IF YOU COULD ONLY X-RAY THESE BAGS!

You know how the voice over the airport PA warns you to check your bags to make sure you've got your own, since so many bags look alike? Well, there's a similar problem at work. It seems like you run into the same types of emotional baggage over and over again. Here are the ones I've encountered a lot. See if they sound familiar.

1. *Mr. Chip-On-His-Shoulder:* This is the guy who could serve as the office's bile refinery. He's carrying a grudge from that promotion he didn't

get, or maybe his kids are driving him crazy. Whatever his problem, he's made orneriness a lifestyle and nothing's gonna change him.

2. *Ms. Know-It-All:* Got a new idea for your department? Don't bother telling her. She already knows all about it. Had trouble with a project? Don't let her find out. She'll say she could have told you it would happen. Few people are as irksome as the colleague who thinks she's got your number. Too bad *her* days aren't numbered!

3. *The Dental Patient:* You're on deadline, you need his input, but getting what you need is like pulling teeth. And while you wait and cajole and bark and moan you watch your deadline slip away.

4. *Ms. By-The-Book:* Has it been approved? Has it been tried before? Does it have a track record of success? There isn't any (heaven forbid) *risk* attached to it, is there? Because if there is, Ms. By-The-Book will filibuster your idea to death. Who needs a boss with her around?

5. *The Firing Squad:* This is the guy who's got a million reasons why it won't work, and he never misses a chance to shoot an idea down.

6. *The Strangler:* This is the gal who squeezes the life out of your projects through sheer incompetence. You do your part, then turn it over to her and next thing you know your baby's on life support.

7. *The Saboteur:* You work your socks off on a project—then someone kills it from inside. You pursue a project in secret—then someone spills the beans. It's The Saboteur: that stealthy, often anonymous co-worker who causes your projects to blow up in your face.

8. *The Helping Hand:* You know her: the one with the invisible sign above her desk: "No problem too big or small." Too bad she's an endangered species.

HOW TO KEEP OTHER PEOPLE'S BAGGAGE OFF YOUR TOES

Maneuvering through these cases can be like flying through heavy turbulence without a seat belt. Fortunately there *are* some ways to smooth the flight. If you can keep your cool—that is, strategize first and then respond—you can probably minimize your bruises.

1. *Find the skycaps.* Just like the airport, most companies have people who are pros at handling people's baggage. They're often receptionists and executive assistants—people who interact with lots of folks and have learned just what pushes their buttons. They're likely to know, for

instance, that Della is just back from vacation and it'll take something big to penetrate her post-beach slumber, or that Joe has put in for a promotion and will do almost anything if it will make him look good to his boss. So nose around and find your local baggage handlers. Then learn their tips. They can spare you a lot of knocks.

2. *Offer to carry your co-workers' bags.* As annoying as your co-workers may be, listen to them occasionally and try to empathize with their problems. Don't give them a lot of time, but if they sense you're an ally, they'll be less likely to drop their bags on your toes. And the more goodwill you spread around, the more you'll have to bank on when the going gets a little rough.

3. *Got a gripe about a bag? Talk to its owner.* It's tough to confront a person who's pushed your buttons—but it's easier than handling the fallout after you've talked to everyone else. Nothing creates turbulence in the office like criticism behind someone's back, so beware the tendency to vent your anger indirectly. As my Uncle Fred used to say, "Always stab your co-workers in the front."

4. *Develop a baggage-handling strategy.* Don't just stumble into your co-workers' bags. Develop a strategy for handling them that will help you minimize your bruises. For example:

- Meeting with *Mr. Chip-On-His-Shoulder?* Listen for a few minutes, then direct him to the task at hand. You probably won't squelch his anger, but your willingness to listen may make you less of a target.
- Meeting with *Ms. Know-It-All?* Pump her for all she knows about everything you're doing. Either you'll learn some useful information, or her ignorance will give you insight into how others see your projects.
- Depending on *The Dental Patient?* If he's not on your team, give him a phony deadline. Tell him you need his input a week before you really do (so you can "incorporate it into your report"). If he *is* on your team and you're supposed to work together, make sure your boss knows that he's the gum in the works.
- Got to get a proposal past *Ms. By-The-Book?* Repackage it. Don't tell her it's new; find ways to describe it as an extension of existing programs. Emphasize the elements the company has successfully tried before, and remind her of similar projects the big execs have lauded.
- Got to face *The Firing Squad?* Cool your jets and listen. Amid his million rejections there's apt to be a worthwhile thought or two. Cull them out and address them: your project will only be strengthened.
- Forced to turn your project over to *The*

Strangler? Ask your boss to assign her work to someone else. Or do her share of the work yourself. Those are the best ways to keep her fingers off your baby.

- Fearful of a run-in with *The Saboteur?* Terrorists often leave clues before they strike: critical comments spread around the office, or veiled threats that "business would be better without this project." Keep your ear to the ground and take those comments seriously. When you locate the source, put as much distance between him and your project as possible. Or, make him an "advisor" to your team. He'll be less likely to destroy something he's helped to build.

- Stumbled across *The Helping Hand?* Buy a lottery ticket because today's your lucky day! Then bring her food and flowers. Take her out to lunch. Thank her more than you think is necessary. And above all, look for ways to return the favor.

Then there's one last thing you need to do, as you drive home at night, fuming over your latest injury in the baggage wars. Remember that, just like Jim and me, you have baggage too. That might not make your situation easier. But it will certainly keep you humble.

The Working Wounded Poll

How do you deal with a difficult co-worker?

Fight 'em, 13%
Charm 'em, 40%
Forget 'em, 46%

Poll conducted at *workingwounded.com*.

from email to *workingwounded.com*

How to Drop a Hint That You Need Some Space

I once had an office mate who drove me crazy. He muttered to himself all the time and constantly interrupted me when I was busy or on the phone. I complained to my supervisor numerous times, but she never agreed to move him, so finally I decided to take the matter into my own hands. We worked in an old 1940s era factory building and this person's desk was directly under a huge ceiling fan dating from the original building. One morning, before he came in, I left an old oily machine nut on his

> desk. During the day, I caught him occasionally glancing up at the fan. The next morning I dropped a rusty bolt on his desk. The next day I left another nut and a screw. On Friday he went to our supervisor and asked to be moved.

The Working Wounded Quotebook

66 99

Do not separate yourself from the community.
HILLEL

HOW TO DEAL WITH POLITICS AT WORK

Dear WW: *The politics in my company are driving me crazy. My projects all have tight time lines and I've got to waste hours getting everyone on my team's buy-in. I'm tired of all the tap dancing and ring kissing. Is there any way to escape company politics?*

BLISTERS ON MY FEET AND LIPS

Dear Blisters,

Recently I was having lunch on a plane when the man sitting next to me started to mutter.

"Good to have you aboard. Now, let's meet some of the oddballs, weirdos and eccentrics you'll be working with."

"Somethin' wrong?" I asked. "I wouldn't feed this to my dog!" he barked. "You really shouldn't think of it as food," I replied. "Think of it as *entertainment:* did getting the silverware out of the plastic bag give you some exercise? Did it distract you?" He looked at me confused for a moment, then smiled as he tore into his salad dressing.

Just as it's a mistake to compare airline food to real food, you need to adopt a new attitude when it comes to politics at work. Instead of seeing it as tap dancing and ring kissing, see it as *the way things get done.* Because that's what it is: the unavoidable side effect of trying to accomplish something with

23

a group of needy, neurotic, ego-driven and otherwise normal human beings. Your challenge is to find a way to master and enjoy it. Geoffrey Bellman's book *Getting Things Done When You Are Not in Charge* (Berrett-Koehler, 1992) has great tips for those of us at the shallow end of the corporate pool who can't just snap our fingers and get our way. I've adapted the tips below from it.

1. *Notice how the most effective people in your company get things done.* My dad was one of the top supply officers in Europe during World War II. When I asked him his secret he replied, "Scotch. My best trade was for a jeep and four heavy winter parkas." Political—you bet, but my dad knew the system and his junior officers didn't freeze. Now, Scotch may not have the currency in your company that it had during the war, but your corporate honchos have figured out some equally effective ways to get what they need. Watch 'em closely and see what you can learn.

2. *Plan for the political consequences of your work.* Since politics is a given, it's naive to think your work will be judged on quality alone. You need to give just as much thought to who will be reviewing it. I knew a foreman once who had this really figured out. He knew his boss's boss hated his guts, so he gave his most important projects to others. That way *his* fingerprints wouldn't be on

them. Someone else got the credit, but his pet projects always survived.

3. *Decide what you will—and won't—do in playing company politics.* Kenny Rogers, one of my favorite management gurus, would have summed it up if *only* he'd sung, "Know when to hold 'em, know when to fold 'em, and know when to update 'em (your résumé, that is)." Ask any corporate gambler—you gotta know your personal limits.

from email to *workingwounded.com*

So What's a Little Bribery Between Co-workers?

You know how some people just get crazy about their coffee mugs? Well, the best workplace prank I ever saw was when a co-worker "kidnapped" another co-worker's mug. She held it for ransom and then sent the owner pictures of the mug being held over a bridge, behind a car tire and in other precarious locations. The owner actually offered $10 to get her $2 mug back!

from email to *workingwounded.com*

A Relative Disaster

I will be PATIENT with my office mate, who just so happens to be the CEO's son. Gee, I wonder how he got HIS job?

HOW TO SURVIVE ON A COMMITTEE

Dear WW: *Recently my boss asked me to sit on a new committee. I work in a warehouse and have never done anything like this before. Any tips?*

NEW TO THE MEET MARKET

Dear Meet,

There's a tree house at the end of my block. It's a regular architectural masterpiece, with gables, shutters and a shingled roof, all suspended between five trees. Or I guess I should say it *was* a masterpiece, because during a windstorm last week the wind pulled the trees in opposite directions and the house came crashing to the ground.

Sort of reminded me of the last committee meeting I attended. Everyone was blowing in different directions, then there was a loud crash and debris everywhere. Unfortunately that's not unusual. Lots of committee meetings go that route because the leader and the members haven't clarified how the committee's decisions will be made. People go into the meetings with different expectations, then crash when it's time to come to a resolution.

You can help minimize that problem by asking the committee leader how decisions will be made. Simply asking the question may prompt her to discuss this with the other members so everyone's expectations are in sync. Knowing the decision-making process will also let you play your cards (and your boss's) most effectively. The following questions can help. They were developed at Intel and were included in an article by Eric Matson in *Fast Company* entitled "The Seven Sins of Deadly Meetings" (April/May 1996).

1. *Will all decisions be made by the committee leader, regardless of members' input?* If so, pay attention

27

during the meetings in case there's some useful information, but don't hustle to get your points across. You'll be talking to a wall.

2. *Will the leader make the decisions using members' input?* If so, advocate strongly for your position. Think of yourself as a consultant to the leader: make a case that will be hard to resist.

3. *Will committee members vote on major decisions?* If so, your task is to influence your fellow members. If necessary, horse-trade, compromise; do what it takes to get the votes you need.

4. *Will a decision require every member's agreement?* Consensus comes from the Latin words *con* and *census* (meaning "you've been conned if you think a roomful of our employees can agree on anything"). Consequently it's not often called for in corporate committees. But if your committee requires consensus your game plan should be this: look for the elements you know everyone can agree to and tie key parts of your agenda to those. Hopefully people will agree to your items in order to get the other things they want.

Knowing how decisions will be made will make you a far more effective committee member. It will also streamline your committee meetings. I guess the moral of this story is: tree houses are for birds— and so are meetings with undefined rules about how decisions will be reached.

from email to *workingwounded.com*

So We Convened a Committee of the Guys and Here's What It Came Up With

I work in aircraft maintenance and some of the guys have a pretty raunchy sense of humor. They also love practical jokes and are merciless with new employees. Well, one day, a new hire showed up on the line and they decided to have a little fun. They made a dummy using a pair of coveralls and boots and put it in the flaps of a DC-8. Then they poured a mixture of ketchup, hot sauce and BBQ sauce on it. At first glance it really looked like a mechanic had been chewed up pretty bad. Well, a short time later the new guy comes out to the plane. He takes one look at that dummy and you could have heard his scream all the way to the next state. I don't think he'll soon forget his first day at work.

The Working Wounded Toolbox

Peer Pleasure . . . How to Get In Sync with Your Co-workers

- Expect not to be appreciated
- Focus on what they know
- Risk being converted by them
- Model the behavior that you want in return

from *Getting Things Done When You Are Not in Charge*
by Geoffrey Bellman (Berrett-Koehler, 1992)

from email to *workingwounded.com*

Weight-ism?

A co-worker once said to me, "I hate your skinny little body. And because you're so skinny, I hate you as a person also!"

HOW TO TELL WHEN A HUSTLE HAS BECOME HARASSMENT

Dear WW: *This guy I've been working with for the last few years has suddenly decided I'm his "dream girl." He's*

constantly sending me lurid love notes and begging me to date him. I'm starting to avoid meetings and hallways where I'm likely to see him, but that's getting in the way of my work. I'm embarrassed and don't know what to do.
                                    JUST TRYING TO SAY NO

Dear Just,

Remember Mitsubishi's old slogan "The word is getting around"? It's taken on new meaning these days—ever since the company was accused of sexual harassment at its plant in Normal, Illinois. Well, it turns out what's "normal" in Normal may have a new meaning for you, too, because the situation you're describing could also be sexual harassment.

Hard to believe? Listen up. The courts today are taking the position that sexual harassment doesn't require a physical assault. It just needs to be "unwelcome" and have a "negative impact." Locker room humor, lewd calendars and, yes, repeated and unwelcome requests have all spawned successful lawsuits.

So you may have a more serious situation than you realize. I'd suggest reading *Step Forward* by Susan Webb (MasterMedia, 1991). It's one of the best primers on recognizing and addressing sexual harassment. The following questions have been adapted from it and should help you decide if the behavior you're experiencing has crossed the line into the harassment camp:

1. *Is the behavior sexual in nature or sex-based?* Clearly fondling has no place at work, but as we said before, behavior doesn't have to be physical to be considered sexual harassment. It can be any comment or joke directed at you simply because of your sex.
2. *Is the behavior deliberate and/or repeated?* Graphic or invasive behavior can happen once and be considered a problem. But less flagrant behavior (like being asked for a date) can be harassment, too—*if* it happens a lot.
3. *Does the behavior affect your ability to work?* You don't have to lose a job or a promotion to have been damaged in the eyes of the court. A negative atmosphere that impedes an employee's ability to work has been legally deemed harassment.
4. *Is the behavior not welcome, not asked for and not mutual?* If you decide this behavior does seem like harassment, and decide to file a claim, the investigator will want to know how you reacted. The theory is "it takes two to tango," and it's important to show that you weren't a willing partner.

Webb suggests starting with the "broken record" approach: saying over and over again, "I don't appreciate it when you say that to me. I don't appreciate it when you say that to me . . ." If that fails, check out your company's sexual harassment policy. You may be able to file a claim in-house, or you may need to hire an outside attorney.

Fortunately, "the word is getting around" about sexual harassment. Thanks to Mitsubishi, what used to be normal in Normal, won't be normal for long.

from email to *workingwounded.com*

Good Thing *This* Isn't Normal Anymore

Twenty-five years ago or so, back in the Stone Age, I had a job which required regular polygraph exams. As I sat there, connected to various wires, the manager giving the test asked, "Do you find me attractive?" "No," I lied, the falsehood obvious as he looked at the needles scratching the paper below him. "Do I inspire sexual thoughts in you?" I told him to cut it out (before the terrible truth machine revealed any more thoughts from that base part of my mind) and the rest of the exam continued without incident. But when I thought about it afterward I got annoyed and quit. A manager with a polygraph is a truly dangerous thing.

The Working Wounded Quiz

Must two employees with the same job title and seniority be paid the same wage?

Answer on page 331.

The Working Wounded Toolbox

But Then I'd Only Stay for Five Minutes . . . How to Survive the Company Picnic

1. After a few beers, switch to soft drinks
2. Don't say things you'll regret back at work
3. Be friendly, but not amorous
4. Avoid skimpy attire
5. Leave while the picnic is still upbeat

from Andrew Sherwood of Goodrich & Sherwood,
via the *Wall Street Journal*

"Whatever makes her think our employee empowerment program confers the right to bear arms?"

HOW TO CONTROL YOUR ANGER AT WORK

Dear WW: *I've always had problems keeping my temper. Last week I blew up at something a co-worker said and pushed him. I was suspended for a week without pay. My boss tells me I have a problem, but I don't know what to do.*

IT'S HIT THE FAN

Dear It's,

Your letter reminded me of a plate glass window that once leaped in front of my hand. Of course, it was the guy in front of it I was aiming for. He'd pushed my buttons once too often and I vowed he'd pay for it—until that window came to his aid. Twenty stitches later I decided that was the last time I'd try to solve a problem with my fist.

I got some slack that time 'cause I was only thirteen. But as you can see from your suspension, adults today get a lot less sympathy for their outbursts. Consider this episode a warning shot across your bow—and look for ways to curtail that fighting instinct in the future. An anger-management program is a good place to start. So is Hendrie Weisinger's book *Anger at Work* (Morrow, 1995). These questions are adapted from it:

1. *Do you really believe you have a problem?* Your letter suggests you may not, but until you do, it can't be fixed. And until your boss and co-workers see you acknowledge your problem, they won't trust you not to explode again.
2. *Do you know how to recognize the first signs of an outburst?* They're probably physical—a tightness in your head, a twisting in your stomach, a clenching of your teeth. You need to create an internal bomb squad that can recognize those signs and quickly defuse your reaction.

3. *Can you learn to defuse quickly?* It might mean taking some deep breaths, or running up and down the stairs—find an outlet that will let you burn off your anger *before* it hits the fan.

4. *Can you identify what provoked you?* Anyone who's tried to quit smoking knows that the temptations of a smoky bar are overwhelming. So it is with anger. As much as possible, avoid the people and situations that have been a problem for you in the past. This may involve sucking up your pride and asking to be transferred to a different project or work area.

5. *Have you investigated better ways to resolve your conflicts?* Perhaps someone in human resources, a.k.a. personnel, is trained to mediate conflicts with colleagues or perhaps you can find a third party who can help. Nonviolent resolutions are out there. Find them.

You know, in earlier days, bosses often excused their workers' outbursts with a grudging "boys will be boys." But those days are gone. Too many workers have "gone postal" and government statistics now indicate that homicide is a leading cause of workplace death. There is zero tolerance for violence in today's workplace. And that raises a final question for you to consider: *In the heat of your anger can you choose to "cool it" in the interest of keeping your job?* Testosterone or a paycheck—you make the call.

The Working Wounded Toolbox

How to Tell When a Co-worker Might "Go Postal"

1. He has explosives tied to his body
2. He begins to burn his office furniture
3. He cc's all letters to the Angel of Death
4. A SWAT team visits frequently
5. He's begun to plan his "Twinkie defense"

from *Going Postal* by Scott Milzer (Villard, 1996)

The Working Wounded Quotebook

Don't wrestle with pigs; you get dirty and the pigs enjoy it.

ANONYMOUS

HOW TO GIVE A SUCCESSFUL APOLOGY AT WORK

Dear WW: *I made a mistake that caused a lot of extra work and problems for one of my colleagues. I'm embarrassed to admit it, and nervous of the consequences, but I* *can't keep avoiding this woman: we're in the same work group. I don't know what to do.*

EGG ALL OVER MY FACE

Dear Egg,

You know how a major U.S. car company once recalled some of its cars and trucks because they'd begun to resemble the Olympic torch? Well, sounds like it's time for you to do a little recall of your own—by fessing up to the little blaze that *you* ignited. I know it's not easy—taking the heat never is, and no one likes to apologize—but it's the only cure for your anxiety, the only responsible thing to do, and the only way to rebuild a relationship that you need to maintain. The trick is to handle the apology well so that you garner the woman's respect rather than her disdain.

In "Go Ahead and Say You're Sorry: Psychological Aspects of Apology" (*Psychology Today,* January/February 1995), Dr. Aaron Lazare offers the following tips to help you frame a constructive apology:

1. *Name your mistake and accept responsibility for your actions.* Leave your spin control and public relations skills back in your office. You need to be prepared to acknowledge your error in terms that show her you know it was a mistake in both your head and your heart. This can be as simple

39

as saying "I screwed up when I estimated that job," or "I should have checked with you before I made that promise."

2. *Show you understand the impact of your error on the other person.* This is the most difficult part. Show her that you've put yourself in her place and understand her feelings. Let her know you realize how much additional work it created—and offer to help her with the burden.

3. *Explain why you did it in the first place.* Here's where most apologies backfire: there's a big difference between giving someone a context for your actions and trying to shift the blame. You may want to practice in front of someone else to be sure you don't add anything that could be considered self-serving.

4. *Express genuine regret for what happened.* That means with the right words and the right delivery. Blurting it out as you race down the hall, sending it email or passing a message through a third party just doesn't cut it. Don't approach her at a time or place that's good for you; approach her in a way that will work for her.

Whatever you do, don't follow the example of former Senator Bob Packwood who was accused of sexual harassment. At his press conference he said, "I'm apologizing for the conduct that it was alleged that I did." To which many people responded, Bob, this is the second time your lips have gotten you into trouble.

from email to *workingwounded.com*

How to Get the Most Mileage out of the People You Work With

I work at a large computer company where people tend to be proud of their consumer-savvy purchases. One of my co-workers bought a new economy car and was boasting about its gas mileage. So we all started taking turns bringing gas for his new car and adding it to his tank when he wasn't looking. As a result he stayed on his first tank of gas for hundreds and hundreds of miles. When he came in to say he was getting great miles per gallon, everyone would give him a hard time.

from email to *workingwounded.com*

Some People Really Know How to Bug You

At Sun Microsystems on April 1, 1986, some employees dismantled a 1966 VW Beetle and reassembled it in someone's office.

The Working Wounded Quotebook

66 99

Nothing so needs reforming as other people's habits.

MARK TWAIN

PUMMELED FROM ABOVE

How to Manage Your Boss

EVER HAD A BOSS YOU WANTED TO STICK PINS IN?

This chapter is about bosses—so I figured, why not start with a little story about voodoo?

My wife, Robin, was in New Orleans a few years ago, and at a friend's suggestion she decided to check out the Voodoo Museum. Unfortunately the directions were as muddy as Cajun coffee and she got totally lost. She stopped an older man on the street and asked, "Do you know where I can find the Voodoo Museum?"

"Voodoo?" The man scratched his head and proceeded to help Robin understand voodoo better than any museum ever could. "I don't believe in no voodoo. That stuff's not real. That stuff were real, you'd read about it, werewolves and devils an'

43

things in the newspapers. But you don't. And anyway, even if it *was* real, I don't worry 'bout it none. You know why? Because I got me a gun—and that's all the protection I need!" He laughed, a great, self-satisfied laugh. "I don't need to worry 'bout no voodoo."

Great, she thought, now I'm lost and I'm talking to a loony packing a .38. Robin said she wished the museum were right in front of her so she could stick a pin into her friend.

"But you know, even if that didn't work, I'm still protected." The man leaned in closer. "You know how?" His gnarled lips came just inches from her nose. "I got garlic. Garlic don't kill 'em. Garlic just . . ." His voice took on a tone of awe. "Garlic make it so they can't *shape-change*. They come in as mist, they gotta *stay* mist. They come in as a werewolf, they gotta *stay* a werewolf. That what garlic do." He looked up and down the sidewalk, as if to make sure he'd not been heard, then took a step away. "But, anyway," he winked at Robin, "I don't believe in voodoo."

Now, you may not believe in voodoo either—but in the course of your career I bet you've seen some shape-changing. Especially when it comes to the people who occupy the corner office. You know the ones I mean: the ones who can change their minds three or four times in a half-hour meeting. Unfortunately since they frown on garlic or guns in the workplace you'll have to use other techniques to manage your boss's shape-changing. Let me give you an example . . .

DO YOU DO VOODOO? YOU DO.

I'll never forget the time my boss at a big insurance company told me he was "a thousand percent" behind my proposal to restructure our department. He even started naming things that were as solid as his support. "The Rock of Gibraltar! Hoover Dam! Elvis Presley fans!" It was corny and I should have known better, but his inclusion of the King made me think he was really behind me this time. So I worked my tail off. I figured from that point on it was *Viva Las Vegas!*

And it was—until his boss found out about our little project. You wouldn't believe how fast his weathervane spun in the opposite direction once the corporate wind started blowing. The restructuring was canceled and I was suddenly working on an important cost-containment project—tracing every long distance phone call made from our department. Goodbye *Vegas;* hello *Jailhouse Rock.*

That wasn't my first experience with shape-changing bosses—and it won't be my last. But in the years since I've figured out how to deal with their ghostly transformations. I use the "shoveling manure" rule. You know the story; it's launched a thousand speeches. There's a little boy digging in a room full of manure. A man walks by and asks, "What are you doing, son?" to which the boy replies, "With all this s———, there must be a pony in here somewhere!"

Well, that's the key to dealing with a shape-changing boss. What looks for all the world like completely erratic behavior, probably has a rhyme and reason—you just can't see it until you do some digging.

HOW TO PIN 'EM DOWN

My Elvis boss, for instance, always came down on the side of what he thought management wanted. Once I realized that, my job became almost easy: all I had to do was anticipate the folks upstairs before I got invested in a project. Then I'd justify my projects by explaining why they'd appeal to senior management, and my boss would almost always agree. (Incidentally, auguring the honchos' preferences turned out to be far easier than I'd expected. Through executive memos, presentations by the bigwigs, the corporate grapevine and talks with old-timers I was almost always able to gather enough tea leaves to make an educated guess.)

Tacking to the winds of management was my boss's pattern, but there are many others. There's:

- The boss who will do anything to avoid a conflict,
- The boss who will do almost anything to make his archenemy look bad,
- The boss whose every decision is driven by stock options,
- The "fad-meister" whose life is ruled by the latest management craze,
- The boss who just wants to be loved, and, of course,
- The glory boss whose only goal is to get mentioned in the newspaper.

Once you've pinned down your boss's pattern, you can tailor your interactions to meet her needs. For example:

- *She hates conflict?* Show her how many people are lined up on her side and present her with concrete strategies for tackling the unavoidable conflicts.
- *He's focused on making his nemesis look bad?* Show him how your project will inflict pain, aggravation, embarrassment or envy.
- *She's crazed about stock options?* Show her how your proposal will drive up the stock price.

- *He's driven by business fads?* Haul in a book that supports your ideas. (Given the mind-numbing array of business titles these days that shouldn't be hard!)
- *She lives to be loved?* Emphasize the employee benefits of the project—and how all the credit will flow directly to her.
- *He's craving recognition?* With all the newspapers, trade rags and cable channels these days, you should be able to find him fifteen minutes of fame somewhere.

A word of warning, though: not every boss has a pattern. There are always those shape-changers who are schizophrenic (or related to the president of the company), and, chances are, you won't find a pattern (or anything resembling intelligent life) in either of them. All you can do is keep digging—and convince yourself that the biceps you build while shoveling will prove useful later in your career.

HOLD THE GARLIC! I *WANT* MY BOSS TO SHAPE-CHANGE!

Then, of course, there are the bosses you wish would shape-change. I had one of those, too. His name was Dick—but we all called him "Cold Shower" because that's what he gave to every new idea that came across his desk. After collecting more bullet holes than a stop sign on a country road, I finally decided to bring him an idea he couldn't shoot down—one of his own. I remembered a story he'd told me in our first meeting, about a program he'd developed once to get every person in his department involved in the strategic planning process. I wrote up the proposal, changed a few of the details, and handed it in with a smile. But I should've known. Dick was such a pro at rejection that he could round-file his own idea! Someday I expect to pick up a dictionary and see Dick's picture next to the word "rigid."

Another variation on the rigid theme is the boss who plays favorites. Elaine comes to mind. During staff meetings she had a perpetual glower on her face—that is, until Kristine spoke up. She'd get positively giddy about whatever oozed from her mentoree's mouth; then she'd make each of us agree to its brilliance. I got tired, after a while, thinking up pseudo-favorable comments, so I adopted the mantra, "Kristine, how do you do it?" Elaine was so busy fawning, she totally missed the sarcasm. She also missed a lot of constructive suggestions because the rest of us gradually stopped volunteering. So much for employee creativity and input.

As crazy as the Dicks and Elaines are, though,

the worst change-challenged bosses are the ones who are stuck: the ones who can't move forward, can't move backward, can't call 911 if their computers catch on fire. My wife had a boss like that. The feds could have used his in-box for the storage of nuclear waste because things went in and were never seen again. Not surprisingly, his employees' initiative also disappeared.

It's tough working for bosses who can't bring themselves to flex or change. Sometimes the best way to get a little shape-changing going is to enlist the help of someone else in the organization. You don't want to appear to be going over your boss's head or behind his back, but if you can get someone your boss respects to advocate—not for you, but for your idea—that may spur a little movement. Another route around a boss's rigidity is to take his idea and gradually make it your own. Start by supporting his idea and showing him you're working to make it happen; once he sees your commitment he may loosen his control. Then gradually introduce elements you think it needs. Tell him you're strengthening his idea to guarantee its success.

Obviously that's not ideal—you'd rather have the freedom and recognition your ideas deserve. But the fact of the matter is, when you're dealing with your boss—whether he's a shape-changer or rigid—you're not dealing with an equal. His spellbook is a lot more powerful than yours, and he's got a heck of a lot more pins. But if you can keep these pointers in mind, maybe you'll be able to work some magic.

HOW TO PUT 'EM UNDER *YOUR* SPELL

1. *Think carefully before you place your pins.* You'll never vaporize him entirely, so aim for smaller changes that you're likely to achieve. Picking your opportunities and weapons carefully will spare you deadly confrontations and increase your chances of success.
2. *Look for places where you're comfortable under his spell.* In even the most ornery relationship, you're bound to agree on some things. Find the common ground, then try to leverage it into larger areas of autonomy.
3. *Don't cast your spells in anger.* You need your wits about you whenever you try to "manage" your boss, so when she starts to make you crazy, find a safe way to blow off steam. When you've cooled down, plan your next move.
4. *Know when it's time to pack up your pins and go.* As you fight for autonomy and recognition, remember: it's only work. Your boss may be a werewolf, but he goes back to his den at night, and so should you.

Of course, sometimes the situation is beyond repair. If you simply can't leave work behind, if your boss is a toothache that will never go away, it may be time to quit. But be forewarned: all bosses have their quirks; there's no assurance the next one will be better. So think carefully before you jump.

And while you're at it, consider your own behavior—because shape-changing isn't limited to bosses. Have you, for instance, ever stood firm behind a decision, only to jump ship quickly when you saw most of your department lean the other way? Or have you ever naysayed a co-worker's idea just because he had the chutzpah to mention it first? Few of us are blemish-free. Maybe what you really need is to take your boss to lunch. Chances are, even if you don't believe in voodoo, you'll find there's garlic enough for both of you.

The Working Wounded Poll

How do you deal with bosses who don't fight fair?

Do what they say, 8%
Fight 'em all the way, 44%
Get out of their way, 47%

Poll conducted at *workingwounded.com*

---

from email to *workingwounded.com*

Who Says There Is No Such Thing as a Free Lunch?

Trying to cut down on cost, my boss had a few of us in the office doing the mass mailings instead of paying a company to send them out for us. He didn't realize that the amount of money he was paying out in hourly wages to have all of us pulled off our regular jobs to do this far exceeded the amount he was trying to save. Being a chronic complainer and perfectionist (or so he thinks), he said when he saw our work, "I sure am glad that I'm not paying for this!"

from email to *workingwounded.com*

Is That a Skeleton in Your Office or Are You Just Glad to See Me?

My boss was always half asleep when he blew by my desk in the morning and tossed a tape for transcription on my desk, then went into his office and closed the door. No "good morning," no "hi," no

> *nothing! One morning I rigged a cardboard skele-*
> *ton to a string, ran the string up through paper clips*
> *across the ceiling and attached it to his office door-*
> *knob. He arrived, tossed me the tape, went into his*
> *office and closed his door. (UP came the skeleton*
> *right in front of him.) He came out of that office*
> *VERY awake, white as a ghost, and NEVER*
> *breezed by without acknowledging me again!*

WHEN YOUR BOSS DRIVES YOU CRAZY

Dear WW: *In my dream last night I killed my boss. Is*
my subconscious trying to tell me something?

PROBABLY UNHAPPY

Dear Unhappy,

With my B in Psych 101, I normally feel qualified to answer questions about work-related
dreams. But in this case, since a homicide is
involved, I think I'll leave the task to the Psychic
Friends Network (or maybe to a really sharp criminal attorney). I *will* wager, however, that you are
unhappy—and I can tell you that you're not alone.

In the best of times, boss relations are a challenge
(and few would argue that these are the best of

"B.J. has a 'hands-on' management style."

times). Many problems can be mitigated, however, with a little "boss management." Not boss manipulation, mind you, but a dedicated effort to maintain clear lines of communication, authority, information and expectation with the person signing your paycheck.

In a book called *Crazy Bosses* (Pocket Books, 1993) Stanley Bing outlines a series of tactics you can use to handle a boss who is crazy—or one who makes *you* that way. I've adapted the following questions from it:

1. *Are you too emotionally dependent on your boss?* If all your emotional eggs rest in his or her basket, you're asking to have them scrambled. Learn how to gain a sense of satisfaction from a job well done, not just from your boss's comments.

2. *Is it possible to just do your job?* Many of us can't just "do" a job—we have to "be" our job. Next time you're at a party listen to yourself: if the only conversation you can sustain is about what you do for a living, it's time to leave your job at work.

3. *Can you do a better job of keeping your cool?* In a heated argument with your boss, he or she will win every time. Your best bet is to stay level-headed, back up your arguments with facts, and know when to take a time-out.

4. *Can you "work his head"? Crazy Bosses* says every boss who is a bully has his fears and smart employees can learn to exploit them. Probably true, although personally, I'd have to be pretty desperate before I'd hike that road.

5. *Are you preparing yourself for the day your boss's job opens up?* Turnover happens. Get a copy of the job description and start gathering the skills you'll need to become your boss's successor. Who knows? Maybe someday someone will be dreaming about you . . .

A couple more points to consider:

1. *When you feel a conflict heating up, trade places.* Look at yourself from your boss's point of view. Are you as blemish-free as you feel?
2. *Do some digging.* A little spadework on your part may turn up additional information, pressure or history that is forcing your boss's hand.

I hope this helps you develop some new strategies for dealing with your boss. But in case you're still struggling with the implications of your dream, remember the words of Bob Dylan: "Don't worry 'bout those dreams, none, they're only in your head."

The Working Wounded Quotebook **" "**

Take calculated risks. That's different from being rash.

GENERAL PATTON

---

from email to *workingwounded.com*

You Won't Believe What My Boss Said This Time!

We are going to continue having these meetings, every day, until I find out why no work is getting done!

What you see as a glass ceiling, I see as a protective barrier.

I know that's how it's supposed to be done, but do it my way.

I didn't say it was your fault. I said I was going to blame it on you.

from email to *workingwounded.com*

If My Boss Only Knew . . .

If my boss only knew that I testified against him before a grand jury!

If my boss only knew that I'd already turned down that other job offer before he gave me the big raise.

If my boss only knew that someone in his department PUT that skunk in his cabin at our company retreat!

WHEN YOU AND THE BOSS DON'T SEE EYE TO EYE

Dear WW: *I'm working on a new product for my company. It's still early, but so far it's not meeting expectations and my boss wants to pull the plug. With just a little more time I think we could have a winner. But my boss says I'm too invested and not seeing it objectively. How do I get him to see it my way?*

SINK OR SWIM

Dear Sink:

Well, I have good news and bad news. Which do you want first?

The good news is that you're right: every new project deserves some slack. I've yet to see one that didn't require its supporters to circle the wagons at some point, in an effort to defend it from ax-wielders. The bad news is, your boss may be right: personal investment may be clouding your objectivity. So the first thing you need to do—before you sacrifice yourself on the altar of pride—is figure out which of you is being more objective.

A good place to start is by examining your boss's track record when it comes to new projects and ideas. To do this you'll want to take the pulse of co-workers, customers and people from other departments—in short, anyone who's seen him in action.

59

It's possible that he's got a fabulous nose for what works, honed through years of experience; in that case, you want to listen to him closely. On the other hand, he may be frightfully risk-averse and just trying to avoid anything different or new. Either way, if you can step back from the product and try to objectively judge your judger, you're likely to glean some valuable information.

The next thing to do is (unfortunately) considerably harder. You need to judge your own objectivity about the project. And since it's almost impossible to do that without some rose coloring getting in the way, you'll need outside help. The following questions, adapted from *Making the Right Decision* by Lee Roy Beach (Prentice Hall, 1993), can help you look honestly at your project. The answers will tell you how hard you want to fight with your boss to save it.

1. *Would you recognize failure if it bit you on the . . . ?* We all spend lots of time dreaming about success and a lot less time developing a clear definition of what constitutes failure. Is your product's "expectation gap" based on failure to meet specific targets, or just on someone's gut feelings?
2. *If you're using the wrong yardstick for evaluation, where can you find a new one?* Perhaps you can justify why current expectations are unrealistic. Who—inside or outside your company—can

help you develop new ones? A manager from a different division? A friend of a friend who evaluates commercial loans for a bank? Comb your network for everyone who might have an educated opinion. Don't look to them for the answer. Just listen closely, because if you're open to their feedback, they could increase your objectivity.

3. *Have you been putting your bad news to work?* In the early stages of a product launch, it's easy to deny bad news ("sales are down because it's new"; "returns are high because customers don't know us yet"). But rejecting bad news is bad business: it robs you of the chance to improve. Did you mine every bit of data for ways to improve? If not, do it now and see what you learn. This will give you concrete ways to prod new life into your product.

4. *If this product were to die, would a piece of you die with it?* My wife reminds me that I once lamented the end of a project, claiming I'd never again find anything as satisfying. Now here I am writing this book, which I have to admit I love. Just goes to show . . .

Hopefully your answers will show that your product should live. If so, you'll have ammunition to use with your boss. Show him the results. Bring in outsiders to argue on your behalf. Then hope that your boss can bend to an argument that has the facts on its side.

If the answers to the questions suggest that your boss is right . . . well . . . that's harder. Give up gracefully and decide to learn from the experience. There's no sense beating a dead horse when what you really need to beat is a retreat. If it's any consolation, you won't be alone in kissing your product goodbye. According to *World Business*, over twenty thousand new products were introduced last year (including my personal favorite, edible deodorant). Most of these products no longer exist. I hope your product doesn't join them, for it saddens me to think of one more product I'll never get to use. Already, just knowing that I've got to face the rest of my life without edible deodorant has got me in the pits.

from email to *workingwounded.com*

Boss Management: A New Niche for Hallmark?

I once had a boss who never had a nice thing to say. But I found a great way to cure him of that habit. I started thanking him every time he said something negative. I sent him gushy thank-you cards that said things like "Just a token of my appreciation for your thoughtfulness in correcting me." Once I brought him flowers with a note that said "Thank you for pointing out my flaws." Once I told him that thanks to his constant corrections I'd begun to discover my inner self. After about a month of that he got the message. His cutting remarks really tapered off.

The Working Wounded List

Great Lies of Management

1. Employees are our most valuable asset
2. I have an open-door policy
3. You could earn more money under the plan
4. We're reorganizing to better serve our customers
5. The future is bright

from *The Dilbert Principle* by Scott Adams
(Harper Business, 1996)

from email to *workingwounded.com*

Freud Never Talked About This Kind of Envy . . .

I've been working in my company for about six months, and it took me only one of those months to discover that I don't like my boss. He's crass and sexist, and expects everyone to laugh at his jokes even when they're not funny (which is most of the time). Fortunately I don't have to deal with him very often because my office is far from his and he gives me a lot of freedom. I figured I could live with the situation. But yesterday that changed. I went up to his office to meet with him. He was sitting at his desk, working away, and on his head was a hat with a pair of stuffed breasts! I didn't know what to say so I didn't say anything—and neither did he. But, I tell you, today I'm looking in the classifieds.

WHEN THE BOSS WON'T LISTEN TO YOUR IDEAS

Dear WW: *I just spent months working on a proposal. My boss took one look at it and shot it down. And this*

PUMMELED FROM ABOVE

"Oh, come on, it's your job to dream of things that never were and ask 'why not?' and it's my job to tell you."

isn't the first time she's done that. She has a habit of rejecting things outright. How can I get her to give me a chance?

CAN'T GET TO FIRST BASE

Dear Can't,

Imagine this scene: There's an old-fashioned TV set, black and white, its picture a little grainy. On the screen a young man, scrubbed and eager, is about to enter his boss's office. "He's gonna love it, Ginger, wait and see!" the young man bubbles.

Then he winks at the secretary and strides purposefully into the office. Moments later he reemerges, crestfallen and shaky. Now the camera pans back, revealing another man, invisible to Bud and Ginger. "Meet Bud," the man intones. "This morning he was full of initiative and good ideas; now he doesn't know what hit him. What Bud doesn't know is that he's just entered . . . the Wounded Zone 9 to 5."

You know the "Wounded Zone 9 to 5": it's that place where you and your boss seem to exist in parallel universes. Where no matter what you do, you just can't seem to get in sync. Like The Twilight Zone, too many forays into the W. Zone and you start wishing you could change the channel.

Well, this time, before you reach for the knob, try taking an alternative view of the situation. In a book called *Intrapreneuring* (Harper & Row, 1985), Gifford Pinchot III offers some great tips on what to do when your boss doesn't listen to your ideas. I've adapted these questions from his suggestions.

1. *Do you know why your idea is being rejected?* Feeling frustrated is the normal way that most of us react to rejection. But right now you need to keep the lid on your feelings and instead engage your boss in a constructive critique of your proposal. Remember this is not a debating class where

you'll score for every point you make; this is feedback where you take notes and try to hear the points your boss is making. The more information you get, the better your chance of bringing your project back to life.

2. *Could you do a better job of presenting your ideas?* I once saw a great project get shot down because of an inappropriate joke made during its introduction to executive management. Only after apologies were made and rings kissed was the project resuscitated. It's remarkable how many great projects get squandered for reasons totally removed from their merits. So ask your boss and other knowledgeable players: "Ideas aside, how could I have strengthened my position?"

3. *Can you build popular support for the idea?* Mention the idea to others in your department who are likely to support it, and ask them to suggest something similar to your boss. Perhaps with a groundswell of support, his feelings will change. (A word of warning, though: tread carefully so you don't appear to be working behind your boss's back!)

4. *Should you find a new sponsor?* If your boss doesn't listen, maybe someone else's will. Ask yourself: will another department gain if this idea is implemented? Then approach the head of that department. Again, this isn't for the politically

fainthearted; you're potentially treading on your boss's toes. But if you're determined, a detour may be the most effective route.

5. *Should you give up?* Sometimes the world (or those who think they run it) simply isn't ready for a great idea. If you've tried the above and the boss still isn't biting, let it go. Put your energy into doing your job and identifying your next idea. Use what you learned this time to make that one an easier sell.

These questions won't derail all future visits to the Wounded Zone, but they'll give you some useful tools for navigating once you get there. And if all else fails, remember that old W. C. Fields line: "If at first you don't succeed, try, try, again. Then quit. There's no use being a damn fool about it."

from email to *workingwounded.com*

And Remember:
The Boss Is Always Right . . .

My boss was telling me how to interview a job applicant. "When someone begins his answer with, 'Well . . . ,'" he said, "it means he doesn't really know what he's talking about." "Oh, really?" I asked, "why is that?" "Well . . ." he began.

The Working Wounded Quiz

Only one of the following six items can be garnished from an employee's paycheck:

1. The value of time taken for meals
2. Student loans
3. The cost of broken merchandise
4. Tools and materials used in the job
5. Required uniforms
6. Cash register shortages and losses due to theft

Answer on page 331.

from email to *workingwounded.com*

But You *Can* Teach an Old Boss New Tricks

When the boss asks you to do something that doesn't seem right, document! When he piddles on you, make sure you have the papers down. A bad boss can be trained just like a dog.

WHEN YOUR BOSS ASKS YOU TO DO SOMETHING YOU'RE UNCOMFORTABLE WITH

Dear WW: *My boss has given me an ultimatum. I have to take action on an issue, but the two alternatives he's presented me with strike me as clearly unprofessional (and possibly unethical). I feel like I'm caught between a rock and a hard place, and I don't know what to do.*

IN A BIND

Dear Bind,

Please remember, I'm an advice columnist not a genie. I can't grant you the three wishes you really want:

1. to be out of this mess;
2. to have a boss who doesn't ask the impossible; and
3. to grant you three additional wishes.

But I can give you some strategies to help you deal with a boss who's pushed your personal limits.

The first thing you need to do is a little investigation of his requests in order to determine your own bottom line. The following questions have been adapted from *How Good People Make Tough Choices* by Rushworth Kidder (Morrow, 1995).

This is an excellent book whose sole purpose is to help people chart a course when there's no clear right answer.

1. *Is it legal?* Obviously, this is the place to start. If you have any doubt about what your boss is requesting, check with your firm's lawyer, an outside lawyer, the bar association or a law school. It goes without saying that a lengthy prison term does not enhance your résumé.

2. *How does it smell?* It may not be breaking the law, but can it still raise a stink? Spouses, cab drivers and bartenders are all excellent judges when it comes to "smell test" issues.

3. *How would these actions look as media headlines?* Unless you're Madonna (who seems to personify the rule that there is no such thing as bad publicity) it's amazing how your perspective can change when *60 Minutes* shows up at the front door.

4. *How would your mother feel about it?* This is the ultimate test—designed to get you out of the corporate mind-set and into a frame that's up close and personal. Don't trust your mother? Imagine describing these actions to someone whose respect you covet. Or stand in front of a mirror and defend them to yourself. Can you look yourself in the eye?

Who knows: maybe you'll be lucky and after taking the legal, smell, headline and mom tests you won't feel so bad about following your boss's orders. If so, anchors aweigh.

If the actions are as questionable as you seem to think, though, these tests won't lighten your dilemma. So now you need some tougher options. Here are some possibilities:

1. Confess to your boss that this particular assignment makes you "uncomfortable." (Most bosses don't respond well to being told they are "unethical.") His response could surprise you. Perhaps he withheld some information that might change your feeling. Perhaps you misunderstood what he was asking you to do.

2. Volunteer for the toughest task in the department if he'll discharge you from this one.

3. Your boss has given you two alternatives, but perhaps there's a third, or a fourth. As Kidder says, we often think we have a *di*lemma when what we really have is a *tri*lemma. Artful probing may reveal other alternatives you'd be more willing to carry out. If you can't create these on your own, ask your boss to do it with you. Together you may find an action you can both feel comfortable with.

4. Get other players involved. If you and your boss can't agree on an action, ask someone from out-

side your department to help. Perhaps someone from human resources, or the union, or an ally higher in the company can offer some guidance.

Of course, all of these options entail an element of risk—especially if your boss is the kind who doesn't take no for an answer. But that takes us back to the "mother test" above. If you don't try these alternatives and just follow his orders, how will you feel next time you look in the mirror?

It's never easy being between a rock and a hard place. But don't despair. If none of these tips seem useful, follow the advice of Mae West, who also knew a thing or two about hard places. "When choosing between two evils," she said, "I always pick the one I haven't tried before."

The Working Wounded Toolbox

How to Prevent Your Boss from Giving You a Heart Attack . . . Learn CPR

Candid—get the reputation for giving honest answers for good news and bad
Positive—always seek to make your feedback constructive

Regular—don't become invisible: in a busy office out of sight is usually out of mind

from *Seven Survival Skills for a Reengineered World*
by William Yeomans (Dutton, 1996)

from email to *workingwounded.com*

My Boss Is the Worst! No, *My* Boss Is the Worst!

My boss always busts us for not working hard enough; then he has his secretary run all over town doing his personal errands!

Recently I bought an expensive gift for a holiday party gift exchange. Then I got stuck with some cheesy piece of crap that I had to act all excited about because it came from my boss.

On more than one occasion my boss ate my lunch, knowingly, without telling me ahead of time, leaving me without enough time to get another one.

The Working Wounded Quotebook

So much of what we call management consists of making it difficult for people to work.

PETER DRUCKER

from email to *workingwounded.com*

If Only We Could Clone 'Em . . .

My best boss was the best because he never checked the counter on the copying machine.

My current boss is the best because he truly understands when I have to stay home with a sick dog.

My best boss could always find humor in everyday situations. One day I was typing and said to him that something was wrong with my computer, I was missing my commas. He said, "Thank God it's not your periods."

CHAPTER 4

BATTERED FROM BELOW

How to Survive Being a Manager

WAY OUT OF THE BOX

Employees—can't live with 'em, can't live without 'em! Kind of reminds me of my five-year-old daughter. (Now, now, don't get me wrong: I'm not suggesting that employees are like children. That would mean that managers are like adults and that's not a leap I'm about to make at this time.) It's just that living with a five-year-old has given me some valuable insights about how to manage actual grown-ups. Take, for instance, the time my daughter, Hallie, got this great idea for a Halloween costume . . .

At least four weeks before Halloween we started reminding Hallie that she'd need to pick a theme for her costume. We knew from previous years that she'd first want to be a bunny, kitty, witch, fairy, princess, ballerina and Vegas show girl before she settled on a final choice. But this time Hallie fooled us: she announced with absolute conviction that she knew exactly what she planned to be—a mermaid with wings.

Oooo-kay. A mermaid with wings. Why not? So my wife sat down to fashion a scaly mermaid's tail and a pair of gossamer angel's wings. The truth of the matter was that we loved the fact that Hallie had thought of a costume that was so completely out of the box. That she wasn't hindered by reality, or by what other children would be wearing, or by what was available by the pallet at Costco. She was her own independent thinker.

Unfortunately, it turned out to be easier to admire her independence in theory than it was in practice. Every night for the week before Halloween my wife burned the midnight oil sewing and stuffing the costume. As I brushed my teeth and climbed into bed I'd hear her muttering downstairs, "If it's so great to have a kid who *thinks* out of the box, why can't we have a costume that *comes* out of a box?" Finally I realized that I'd better get out of bed and lend a hand lest I myself might be severely downsized.

But as we sat at the kitchen table stuffing wads of newspaper into the mermaid's tail, I realized that

Hallie had taught me something valuable about employees. She was exactly the kind of employee we all want: smart, creative, experimental; high on initiative, strong on project ownership, determined to take the right road rather than the easiest. But nurturing those traits took effort! And the same is true for employees. If we want their good ideas, if we want their initiative and project ownership, if we want their willingness to do more than the bare minimum, then we have to give *them* extra effort, too. We have to give them room to experiment (even if their ideas seem odd at first). We have to praise their efforts (even when they mean extra work for us). We have to invent and sew and paste to get them the resources they need and to clear obstacles from their path. Above all, we have to treat them as individuals; we can't force fit them into costumes out of a box.

Unfortunately, doing that isn't easy—in part because by the time we've made it into management we've bought into the greatest charade of all: the notion that managers are in control. Hah! What could be further from the truth? The only thing you're in control of is your schedule (and sometimes not even that)! The employees (whom you thought you would control) have got you over a barrel because they're the ones who do the work that you get held accountable for! A Russian czar once said: "I don't rule Russia: ten thousand clerks do." Well, he told it like it is.

WHO SAID BOSSES HAVE TO BE BOSSY?

I learned how dependent I was on my employees from a woman old enough to be my grandmother and who fancied herself the toughest granny in the district. Virginia was a volunteer in a nonprofit program I once ran that trained seniors to teach other seniors to protect themselves from crime. "If anyone attacks me I just hit 'em with my cane!" she'd declare to roomfuls of octogenarians, and I'd think, *Great, that's all I need: to have some frail older woman beaten by an assailant using her own cane.* But how could I say that to Virginia? She was so enamored of her routine, and her zest for the program was bringing other seniors in; I couldn't afford to lose her. I struggled for days with how to tell her to stop. Finally, at a loss, I laid the problem at her feet. "Virginia," I said, "what about other seniors, not as strong as you, who might be endangered if their attackers grabbed their canes?" Virginia looked at me wide-eyed as if she suddenly held the lives of those seniors in her hand. "I don't know," she said, "but I'll think of something!" And sure enough, the next day she came back with a solution. "If someone attacks you you'll *wish* you could hit him with your cane!" she said, whacking an imaginary assailant across the knees, "but that's *not* the thing to do." She then gave standard tips for protecting yourself from harm, using her cane for humorous punctuation.

I was blown away. I'd assumed that as the boss it was *my* job to control the situation; to create and impose the solution. But Virginia had come up with a better solution than I ever could have, and in the process she'd boosted her confidence and commitment to the program. She'd taught me the key to managing people!

HOW TO KEEP YOUR PEOPLE IN THE FAST LANE

Of course, if you prefer the "command and control" approach to management, you can always emulate Bonnie. Bonnie ran a department of fifty-two people and ran it with an iron fist—because she had a single abiding fear. She was terrified that she would meet her boss on the elevator and he would ask a question about one of her staff that she wouldn't be able to answer. So to make sure that never happened, Bonnie limited her employees to work she could fully control. No one was allowed to initiate an idea, or try a new approach, or move forward on a project without first discussing it at length with her. The result? You guessed it. People stopped taking initiative. Workers who had formerly had good ideas, who had been eager to "own" their jobs, began to cool their jets and spin their wheels. Bonnie was like one of those entrance ramps on the highway where three lanes merge into one. No matter how much horsepower her employees had, she slowed 'em to an idle while she "stayed on top of" her department.

Maybe Bonnie's problem was that she was laboring under the wrong metaphor. If she'd thought of her employees as *race cars* (instead of as five-year-olds?) she might have been a better manager. She might have given them fuel instead of withholding her support; she might have cleared obstacles from the track instead of standing in their path; she might have focused on the finish line instead of sweating the details at every lap. But alas, she didn't. Eventually she quit her job and went back to school in pharmacology. (Now she'll be depressing people in a whole new way.) But you can learn from Bonnie's errors. If you want to get the most mileage out of your employees, just ask yourself the following questions:

1. *Do they know where the finish line is?* Remember the "missile gap" back in the 1960s? Well, these days many of us are sweating an *expectation* gap: managers expect employees to know their expectations without ever telling them directly. So be realistic: your employees can read your mood; they can read between the lines; but they can't read your mind. Make sure your goals and time lines are clearly spelled out whenever you give an assignment.

2. *Do they have adequate fuel?* My brother says that when he was a rookie lawyer his firm had the uncanny ability to give him just enough information to make him look totally incompetent. If they'd given him more, he'd have been able to do the job exactly the way they wanted. If they'd given him less, he'd have had to figure it out on his own. But they gave him just enough information to maximize his errors. Don't make that mistake with your employees. *Ask* if they have all the information and resources they need, then get them what they're lacking. *You're* the pit crew; *they're* Mario Andretti.

3. *Have you removed the roadblocks from their path?* W. Edwards Deming, the business gurus' guru, said that 94 percent of a company's problems stem not from the people but from the "system." So what can you do to streamline the system for your workers? Start by viewing the system from

their perspective. What red tape is slowing them down? How can you clear it away to save them time and effort? In short, how can you use *your* power and leverage to make *them* more productive?

4. *Do you hand out trophies when they cross the finish line?* A job well done is its own reward, right? So how come the big execs take home hefty bonuses each year and only the employees are supposed to be satisfied with intrinsic motivation? Find a way to reward your employees in the ways that count: cash, stock, time off and/or promotions. For instance, create a bonus system within your department, or use a year-end budget surplus to create a departmental profit-sharing plan. (Who said you can't? Have you tried?) If you can't give them money, then give them time: a day off when they finish an important project; time to regroup after a grueling bout of work. But don't just work off my list: ask what rewards would motivate *them*. And above all, sing their praises—loudly, clearly and repeatedly—*every* time they do good work.

Of course your employees aren't really race cars; they're people. But if you do all these things, you'll probably keep them out of the pits.

The Working Wounded Poll

How do you feel about video surveillance of employees at work?

Hidden cameras are all right by me, 16%
Cameras are fine, but only in places you can see, 36%
No videos at all is my plea, 46%

Poll conducted at *workingwounded.com*

from email to *workingwounded.com*

What Goes Around Comes Around

I've managed people who were older than I was and more talented, but the hardest thing is to manage someone who is smarter. I have an employee now who is half my age and has twice my brainpower and she terrifies me! My husband has to make me go to work in the morning because I just don't want to go. But you know what the worst of it is? For years I enjoyed working my way around bosses who I thought were not as smart as I was, and now here I am—the dumb boss!

---

66 99

If the only tool you have is a hammer you tend to see every problem as a nail.

ABRAHAM MASLOW

THE BEST PLACE TO START SOLVING A PROBLEM ISN'T ALWAYS WITH THE SOLUTION

Dear WW: *I manage a warehouse that's got a huge turnover problem. It's gotten so bad that I've got to run a new employee orientation every other week. I've tried everything I can think of, but I'm starting to think that people just don't want to work anymore.*

TURNOVER BLUES

Dear Blues,

I generally reserve my intimate dental secrets for my dentist, but in this case I'll make an exception. Here's the skinny: I still have a baby tooth—and a while back it thrust me into dental hell. A new dentist, to whom I'd gone for a routine cleaning, declared that the "baby" was disrupting my entire bite and that the problem would cost thousands to fix.

"I'm a great believer in keeping a clean desk, chief."

I didn't bark about my bite. I did what any dental-fearing person would do: I got a second opinion. Dentist No. 2 agreed there could be a problem, but suggested that we monitor the situation for a while. That was ten years ago and the "baby" is still happily nuzzled amidst my molars.

Now, the trouble with the workplace these days is that too many people are like Dentist No. 1. They leap to immediate solutions. Don't get me wrong: there are plenty of times when immediate action is required. But often leaping to solutions only makes things worse. In *Doing It Right the First Time* (Wiley, 1996), Gerard Nierenberg suggests a five-step medical model for diagnosing and treating problems. I've borrowed (even more liberally han usual) from his model.

1. *Are you treating the symptom or the problem?* You claim turnover is your problem. But I suspect that's merely the *symptom* of an underlying disease. Something is causing the turnover, and until you find out what that is, you're just sticking on Band-Aids. So now it's time to run some tests. Poke, prod, question and X-ray your employees until you find out why they're leaving. Could be an unfair supervisor, unrealistic wages, inadequate training . . . Don't stop testing until you've uncovered the root cause.

2. *How should you treat the problem?* This is the *really* hard part. (It's where Dentist No. 1 failed.) Once you've pinpointed the cause, resist the urge to leap to a solution. It won't be the best, only the first. Instead, do some research. Look for alternatives. Ask the people involved to help you come up with solutions. Then work with them to weigh the pros and cons of each. Taking a little longer to get the *right* solution will spare you a lot of pain later.

3. *How can you prevent a recurrence?* As you consider possible solutions, keep in mind that you'll prob-

ably need two: a short-term solution to fix the immediate crisis, and a long-term solution to solve the underlying problems. Resist the temptation to stop at solution number one: without complete treatment, the disease is likely to recur.

So remember: the next time you plan to sink your teeth into a problem, take time for a thorough diagnosis. It will make for better solutions—and save you thousands in dental bills.

from email to *workingwounded.com*

The Challenges of Managing a Mature Workforce

We recently hired an older worker, Rose, as our receptionist (she's sixty-four). Since she'd never worked before I was a little concerned about how she would work out and how she would fit in with our mostly younger employees. As it turns out I was worried about the wrong things. At Christmastime we scheduled a holiday party which was supposed to start right after work. But when I returned from lunch I had quite a surprise. Rose had decided to start the party early. She was up on her desk stripping!

The Working Wounded Quotebook

Keep the five guys who hate you away from the five that haven't made up their minds.

CASEY STENGEL

The Working Wounded Toolbox

It's the Employees, Stupid . . . What Nonfinancial Measures Matter to Institutional Investors

1. Strategy execution
2. Management credibility
3. Quality of strategy
4. Innovativeness
5. Ability to attract talented people

from "What Analysts Really Want"
by Lori Calabro (CFO, December 1996)

HOW TO TELL AN EMPLOYEE SHE MADE A MISTAKE

Dear WW: *Recently one of my people made a mistake and I blew up in her face. Two weeks later she quit.*

Looking back I realize that I overreacted. How can I prevent this from happening again?
EVEN BOSSES GET THE BLUES

Dear Blues,

When it comes to employee screw-ups, I think there are two types of bosses in the world: the "Homers" and the "Cliffs." The Homers (as in Simpson) yell first and investigate later. The Cliffs (from the old Cosby show) investigate so long you wish they *would* yell. It appears that you were listening to your inner Homer when you reacted.

Now, I like spending quality time with Homer and Cliff as much as the next guy, but I'm not sure I'd want to work for either one. The best bosses that I've had turn employee mistakes into learning opportunities. So next time you discover a mistake by one of your people take a deep breath and try asking yourself the following questions:

1. *Does the worker know she made a mistake?* Now, the engineers at Chernobyl *knew* they'd made a mistake. But most employee errors don't result in that kind of meltdown (short of their boss's, that is). So don't assume she knows about her misstep. Ask her how she views the situation—then explain why there's a problem.
2. *Do you know why she acted as she did?* Go back with her to the moment of decision. Listening to

her reasons will show you how she thinks, how she perceives her responsibility and authority, how she perceives *you*. A small amount of corporate anthropology here will teach you both a lot.

3. *Does she understand the ramifications of her action?* To you they're self-evident: *your* boss is ragging on *you;* the crucial deadline is likely to be missed; there's going to be a loss where a profit was supposed to be . . . But she probably doesn't have access to that data. We often expect employees to understand the consequences of their actions without giving them the information they need to do so.

4. *Did the employee understand your expectations?* Often mistakes are made because employees are trying to second-guess you. Had you communicated exactly what you wanted? Made it clear where her authority stopped? Indicated your willingness to help? Communicating these things now can forestall disasters in the future.

5. *Have you explained how you'd like to see the problem fixed?* There's nothing worse for an employee than trying to fix a mistake only to dig the hole deeper. So take the guesswork out of the repair business and walk her through the steps. She'll learn valuable bits of your business in the process.

All of these tips really boil down to communication—making your expectations clear, keeping the channels open, getting feedback from employees so you know how they perceive the situation. (It also helps to remember the employee point of view. For a crash course, check out *Rivethead* by Ben Hamper, Warner, 1991.) The alternative, of course, is to keep pulling a Homer. But you may find after a while that there's no one left at home. Not even your inner Marge.

The Working Wounded Quotebook   **" "**

The essence of genius is knowing what to overlook.

WILLIAM JAMES

The Working Wounded List

You Think You've Got an Employee Who's a Loser? Check Out These Guys!

1. Yasuo Hamanaka, a trader for Sumitomo in Japan, tried to corner the worldwide market on copper and instead lost $1.8 billion.

2. Nicholas Leeson, a trader for Barings Bank in Singapore, invested in derivatives and lost $1.3 billion.
3. Toshihide Iguchi, an investment banker from Daiwa Bank in Japan, made a bad currency bet with U.S. Treasury Bonds and lost $1.1 billion.

from the *New York Times* (June 16, 1996)

from email to *workingwounded.com*

People Who *Really* Need People . . .

I once asked one of my employees to stop reading a People *magazine at her desk and to get back to work. She began to cry and went out on disability for two days.*

HOW TO FIRE AN EMPLOYEE

Dear WW: *One of my managers wants to fire a person in his department. I ran it by our company lawyer and he's concerned that the employee has a file full of good to*

*excellent recommendations. Are we asking for trouble if we
fire an employee with consistently good evaluations?*
                    BETWEEN A ROCK AND MY LAWYER

Dear Rock,

Did you ever hear about "dishwasher fish"? The
spicing may vary but the cooking method's always
the same: wrap the fish in tinfoil, put it in the dishwasher and run it through a cycle. Voilà: a perfectly cooked fillet. (And just think how good you'll
feel when dinner is ready and there are no dirty
dishes.)

Well, your letter got me thinking about dishwasher fish and how much we all love a good
shortcut. Unfortunately when it comes to firing an
employee, most shortcuts lead to the same place.
Can you say "wrongful termination lawsuit"?
Because while it's true that managers can fire
nonunionized employees "at will" (that means
without giving a reason), the majority of employees—women, minorities, the disabled and anyone
over forty—are legally protected from such an
action.

So how *do* you fire someone without leaving a
blood trail for the lawyers? Linda Walton, an
employment attorney for Seattle-based Helsell,
Fetterman, says (paraphrasing that old retail saw),
"documentation, documentation, documentation."
When her corporate clients say, "That was the last

straw; I just had to fire him!" she responds: "if that was the *last* straw, what were straws one, two and three?" Before you fire someone from a protected class or a union, make sure you've built a case for your decision. She suggests you start with the following questions:

1. *Do your managers handle employee evaluations honestly?* Or do they rate all their employees "excellent"? Chances are your employees are good . . . but not *that* good. Require your managers to evaluate both their strengths and weaknesses, and be sure that excellent evaluations are not handed out like penny candy.

2. *Do you require documentation for all lapses in employee performance?* "If I told her once, I told her a million times . . ." just doesn't cut it in court. Your managers need to describe *in detail* all performances that are substandard, and then include those reports in employees' personnel files. Anything short of complete and specific documentation can mean that poor performers get the equivalent of lifetime employment.

3. *Do you hold your managers accountable for proper evaluation and documentation?* I asked Walton what to do when you want to fire an employee who lacks a documented record of poor performance. Her reply: "Start with the bigger problem: fire the incompetent manager first."

So it sounds like you've got your work cut out for you if you really want to fire that employee. Assuming, of course, you don't want her lawyers making dishwasher fillet out of you.

from email to *workingwounded.com*

Should This Employee Be Canned?

I manage a flower shop. Once I wrote on the delivery slip, "<u>can</u> leave on porch." (For emphasis I underlined "can.") About an hour later the delivery driver came back to the shop in a panic and began looking all over the shop. I asked her what she was looking for and she replied, 'I can't find the can! It's getting late and I have to get this delivery done!' "What can?" I asked. "The can to leave on the porch." Needless to say, I now write, "You may leave the flowers on the porch if the customer isn't home."

The Working Wounded Quiz

You fired an employee for poor performance, which you believe was the result of a drinking problem. If you are specifically asked about it, can you tell that to a prospective employer during a reference check?

Answer on page 331.

The Working Wounded Quotebook

What is honored in a country will be cultivated there.

PLATO

AS A NEW MANAGER, HOW CAN I MAKE MY MARK?

Dear WW: *I just got a big promotion to be the manager of my department. I thought everybody would rally around me as a former employee, but instead it feels like an invisible wall has gone up all around me. Are there some things I can do to show them I'm going to be a different kind of boss?*

STILL THE SAME OLD JOE

Dear Same,

Recently my five-year-old daughter, Hallie (a veritable font of business insight), announced that she knew what she was made of. "Snakes and snails and puppy dog tails?" I teased. "No," she said derisively, "that's *boys*. *I'm* made of skin and bones and imagination!"

Well (again, not wanting to draw *too* close a parallel between my daughter and your career) it strikes me that there's a certain similarity between her sense of anatomy and your new job. That is, you seem to have captured the "skin and bones" of the people who report to you (their bodies show up for work), but you haven't yet fired their imaginations by showing them what an inspiring leader you can be.

Unfortunately that's not something a promotion automatically drops in your lap. It's something you've got to earn. Hopefully the following tips (adapted from *Flight of the Buffalo* by James Belasco and Ralph Stayer, Warner, 1994) will help:

1. *Are you giving your workers the responsibility AND authority they need to do their jobs?* Don't make that old mistake of expecting your workers to win the race while *you're* pulling back on the reins. The best thing you can do to prove you're a different kind of boss is to set the standards high—

then give your employees room to decide how to get those standards met.

2. *Are you a good coach?* And I don't mean the kind of coach who barks, "Drop down and give me twenty (push-ups)." You want to prove to your employees that you're genuinely interested in their development. Jointly develop a "skills improvement plan" with each employee and meet regularly to review each person's progress. Annual reviews are a joke; you should be talking with your people *monthly* about their strengths and weaknesses.

3. *Have you shown your employees that you're attentive to their concerns?* Managers expect people to jump at their orders—but few managers set records when it comes to responding to their employees' wishes. If you want to be respected, walk your talk. Make your corner of the bureaucracy more responsive to the people who report to you.

The fact is you *aren't* the same old Joe anymore because, like it or not, you're now signing paychecks. But one thing hasn't changed: your ability to see the obstacles you saw so clearly when you were on the other side. And that gives you your biggest chance to tear down that invisible wall: you can use your power as a manager to do something about the bureaucratic folderol that drives employees mad. It may not be easy, but if you just use a lit-tle imagination . . .

The Working Wounded Toolbox

Don't Know How to Coach the Best Effort from Your People? Start by Asking Them . . .

1. In the best of all possible worlds, what is great performance for your customers?
2. What do you want to achieve in the next two to three years?
3. How will you measure your performance?
4. What things do you need to learn in order to reach your goals?
5. What work experiences do you need to help you learn what you need to achieve your goals?

from *Flight of the Buffalo* by James Belasco and Ralph Stayer (Warner, 1994)

from email to *workingwounded.com*

Managers' Dirty Little Secrets

*If only my employees knew that I ran out of money
to pay them two weeks ago :)*
*If only my employees knew that I have no clue how
to run this place!*

HOW CAN I MOTIVATE MY EMPLOYEES ?

Dear WW: *I'm looking for a way to motivate my
employees and a friend suggested a contest. But it sounds
hokey to me. Do contests really work?*

BABY, CAN I LIGHT THEIR FIRE?

Dear Baby,

You've obviously never entered Publishers
Clearinghouse. You bet contests work—but you
gotta do 'em right. Not like the bank that someone
recently emailed me about that ran a motivational
contest. Grand prize was . . . (*drum roll*): dinner at
the bank! Now, I don't know about you, but when
I think about award-winning dining, I don't exactly think BANK.

"All right, everybody, recess is over!"

Then there was the high-tech company that ran a contest challenging employees to find the bugs in a new piece of software. Only problem was, they ran the contest before the software was finished. Uh, guess what happened? Three employees put bugs in the product just so they could find them. (Now they might be nerds, but they're no dummies.)

So your friend's got the right idea—you just have to do it right. The following questions, adapted from *Management Would Be Easy . . . If It Weren't for the People* by Patricia Addesso (AMACOM, 1996), will give you some pointers:

1. *What exactly are you trying to encourage?* Make sure your contest rewards the right behavior. Bugs *out* of the program—not in it. That software company should have offered to reward employees who *created* a bug-free program, not the ones who cleaned up the mess. It sounds obvious, but take the time to figure out exactly the kind of behavior that you want before you start handing out prizes.

2. *Do employees value the prize you're offering?* There's only one sure way to come up with a great prize: ask the people you're trying to motivate. (Who knows? Maybe they'll *want* a dinner at a bank.)

3. *Is the contest outcome tied to performance or to chance?* One small company I know created an Employee of the Month program, hoping to motivate outstanding performance. Trouble was, they created a lottery instead—by failing to create measurable standards for winning (such as dollar sales or evaluations from customer comment sheets). As a result, any employee was eligible to win. And sure enough, after the first few months (wanting to preserve the company's "family atmosphere" and prevent hard feelings) the owner felt the need to spread the winning

around. The program became a joke as employees merely waited for their turn to win.

4. *Do employees believe they have a chance of winning?* One manager told me about a contest he's run that no employee has ever won. "I haven't given anything away in four years," he bragged. I bet his employees aren't giving much either.

So to answer your question—"yes!" Contests *can* be great at lighting a fire—if they're well designed. The trick is to make sure you're not the one who gets burned.

The Working Wounded List

Employee Hierarchy of Needs

Level 6 (highest level)—More money
Level 5—False hope of advancement
Level 4—Recognition
Level 3—Thrill of empowerment
Level 2—Artificial challenge created by poor
planning and inadequate resources
Level 1 (lowest level)—Coffee, donuts,
caffeinated soft drinks

from *Dogbert's Top Secret Management Handbook*
by Scott Adams (Harper Business, 1996)

from email to *workingwounded.com*

More Dirty Little Secrets

If only my employees knew that I am not working here at my desk; I'm really Web surfing!

If only my employees knew that I listed them all as unlimited partners when I filed the company income tax!

If my employees only knew that I had one testicle. (Hey, don't blame Working Wounded—we don't write 'em, we just report 'em.)

The Working Wounded Quotebook

66 99

You've got to give loyalty down if you want loyalty up.

DONALD REGAN

IS MY CONSULTANT GETTING THE JOB DONE?

Dear WW: *I just took over the management of a manufacturing plant and discovered I've inherited two consultants. Neither is on a long-term contract and I'm* *wondering if there are any accepted ways to evaluate consultants to decide if I should keep them on the pay-roll?*

FISH OR CUT BAIT

Dear Fish,

I'm a sucker for a great slogan, and I saw the best slogan ever while driving on a country road a few years back. It was on a sign that advertised a combination veterinarian/taxidermy shop. Written in red script across the bottom of the sign were the immortal words, "Either way you'll get your pet back."

I always think of that sign when the subject of consultants comes up. For one thing, in today's downsized workplace, consultants are multiplying faster than rabbits. For two things, they often do little more than add insult to injury. But then, consulting isn't the world's third oldest profession for nothing. There *are* times when a consultant can provide insight, special expertise or an extra set of hands to tackle a difficult problem. So you're right to evaluate the usefulness of your pair. The following questions, adapted from *The Manager's Desk Reference* by Cynthia Berryman-Fink and Charles Fink (AMACOM, 1996), should help:

1. *Do the skills provided by the consultants already exist within your organization?* If so, no point paying outsiders. Especially since nothing deflates employees' tires more than feeling sidestepped in

the search for solutions. So see what you've got in-house before committing to the "experts."

2. *Have these consultants been earning their keep* recently? If there's one question to ask a consultant it's "What have you done for me lately?" Then demand specific answers. If what they say smacks of sizzle, but lacks the steak, it's probably time to part ways.

3. *Are your consultants tailoring their solutions to your needs, or have they got you in a one-size-fits-all package?* Generic solutions aren't much good when you've got customized circumstances and problems. So make sure you're getting what *you* need—not just what they can offer.

4. *Are your expectations realistic?* As you evaluate their performance, keep in mind that you're working with consultants, not Mother Teresa. If your company was a mess, they may legitimately need more time to achieve results (although you should be seeing signs of progress). Make sure you're providing them adequate support—then expect progress, but not a miracle.

5. *Is the company becoming dependent on the consultants?* If they're providing skills you need on an ongoing basis, either bring 'em in-house or have them train your people. You want to *own* the skills you need for daily operation.

I hope that helps. Evaluating consultants is not always easy. But I think if you listen to the Finks your consultants won't put you in a funk.

from email to *workingwounded.com*

Michael's Silver Hammer Came Down Upon His (and Our) Head

I saw this joke in Readers Digest. An optimist sees the glass as being half full, a pessimist half empty, while the reengineering consultant observes that you have 50 percent more glass than you need.

from email to *workingwounded.com*

Even More Dirty Little Secrets

If only my employees knew that I take credit for their ideas and then take the bonus checks they would have earned for them.

If only my employees knew that the managers' restrooms have cable TV and complimentary snacks and soft drinks, then they'd understand my "chronic stomach problems."

The Working Wounded Quotebook

You do not lead by hitting people over the head—that's assault, not leadership.

PRESIDENT DWIGHT EISENHOWER

CHAPTER
5

SQUEEZED INTO A BOX

How to Get Ahead

TURNING MOLEHILLS INTO MOUNTAINS

Do you ever feel like your career is stuck, like one of those ancient metal desks that take two bodybuilders to move? Well, my wife had an encounter with a desk like that, and it taught us something valuable about moving ahead at work.

At the time, Robin worked in a midsized company where she managed a young woman named Leslie. When Robin arrived at the company, Leslie was working in a corner of the break room. At all hours of the day, her office was filled with the laughter and lamentations of her co-workers who were only too eager to lure her into conversation. Needless to say, it was not a work-conducive environment.

"We need to find you a new office," my wife noted her first day on the job.

"Oh, I have a new office," Leslie responded. "It's right around the corner. I'm just waiting for the interior designers to decide where the furniture should go before I can move in."

"You can't decide yourself where the furniture should go?"

"Oh no," Leslie shook her head. "Howard [the CEO] would never allow it."

Well, a week went by, then a second week, and Leslie's new office sat vacant. My wife asked her own boss about moving Leslie in, but he echoed Leslie's words: Howard wouldn't allow it. So another week passed, and another, and gradually my wife began to think that Leslie would never move. Then, one day, as she was walking down the hall, she heard men's voices coming from the unused room. She looked in and sure enough, there were two burly workmen unrolling a set of architectural plans. As she watched, they laid the drawings on the floor, compared them to the layout of the room, then moved the desk six inches to the right. They stepped back for a moment to admire their handiwork, then they rolled up the drawings and left the room.

My wife stood in the hall, stupefied. For *this* they had waited four weeks and spent who knew how much money? Apparently so—for the next day she received a note from Howard: "Office ready. Tell Leslie to move in."

My wife left that job a few months later, and for years we told that story to friends, only to have them laugh and shake their heads in disbelief. But as I sat down to write this chapter it occurred to me that this kind of incident is far more common than we'd thought. It's not that companies are trying to pull a "Martha Stewart" when it comes to arranging their employees' offices. It's that the saga of Leslie's desk is the perfect metaphor for how companies deal with *employee advancement*. They don't move you when you've outgrown your job; they do it when they've got a space available. They don't ask you for input; they make all the arrangements for you. And when they do get around to moving you, they do it in six-inch increments, not the leaps you had in mind. Let's face it: when push comes to shove, the average company is more concerned about the angle of your desk than about the trajectory of your career.

AT LEAST YOU CAN TAKE THE TOOTH FAIRY TO THE BANK

Now, to be fair, I've heard that there *are* companies that mentor, counsel, train and support the growth and development of their employees. I've also heard that there's a tooth fairy. The only difference is, I once got a quarter from the tooth fairy and I have yet to see people whose career development was really supported by their employer. Oh, sure, companies talk a good line: "Our people are our greatest asset" is a common slogan. Unfortunately, it's rarely translated into their investment strategy.

So what does that mean for you? It means that *you* have to assume the leadership of "You, Inc." (After all, if you take the "You" out of "You, Inc." you're left with "Inc.," which, in my experience, means "incomplete." And I should know because in college I collected "Inc.'s" the way my buddies collected beer bottles.) How do you manage "You, Inc."? You do it as if you were the world's most valuable property. You develop a strategic plan; you draft a board of advisors; you put time and money into R&D . . . In short, you determine where you want to go and what you'll need to get there. Then you pursue those goals the way you used to pursue Boardwalk in Monopoly.

In fact, building your career is a lot like playing Monopoly. Remember how you'd wheel and deal, collecting properties and building hotels, trying to wipe out your opponents? Well, advancing your career is similar (though hopefully not so ruthless). You decide which assets will advance your career, then you navigate the workplace world to get them. If you're strategic in your choices, they'll give you a heck of a return on your investment.

CAREER MONOPOLY

Here are some tips for playing Career Monopoly:

1. *Pick your strategy: Baltic or Boardwalk?* You know how after you played the same opponents a few times you began to recognize their strategies? There were those who always went for the expensive properties: Boardwalk and Pennsylvania Avenue. They hoped to decimate your savings with a few well-chosen sites. Then there were those who took the "more is better" route: they bypassed Boardwalk and Pennsylvania but tried to buy up all the lavenders, pinks and purples, hoping to nickel-and-dime you to death on every move. Well, like those childhood players, you need to develop a strategy for how you're going to get a monopoly on your career. You need to decide where you want to end up, then scout out all the options that could help get you there: degree programs, professional training courses, strategic volunteering, finding a mentor . . . Decide which are best for you (which fit your needs, budget and lifestyle), then plan how you'll pursue them over the next five to ten years.

2. *Advance to Go. Collect $200.* Remember how the game gave you free money every time you passed Go? Well, there may be "free" money in

your workplace that you can use for career advancement. Once you decide what courses you want to take, talk to your supervisor or human resources department. Even companies that don't advertise their willingness to pay for training will sometimes do so if you can make a case that your training will benefit the company. If your company won't pay for coursework, see if they'll allow time off for volunteering. Show them how the time will enhance your skills.

3. *Take advantage of Free Parking.* Free parking was the one "safe" space on the board where you didn't have to worry about making a decision, or paying rent, or suddenly ending up in jail. It gave you a chance to rest and take stock of the situation before moving on. Wouldn't it be nice to have that same kind of respite in the world of work? A place where you can step out of the politics and hustle of your day-to-day job and gain a different perspective? Well, you can. It's called finding mentors: people whose wisdom and skills you value and who would be willing to take the time to pass them along. Well-selected mentors can coach you on advancing your job skills, or on scouting your next advancement; they may even be able to chaperone your climb up the ladder. Look for people with demonstrated political savvy and expertise in areas you want to learn. Mentors can be inside or outside your

company, and can change as your skills and needs advance. Once you've identified a potential mentor ask them if they'd be interested in joining the board of directors of You, Inc. Tell them the pay is lousy, but the perks are great (lots of chances to talk with you).

4. *Don't stop at houses; go for hotels.* I had a serious fault as a Monopoly player. As soon as I bought a property I'd get distracted by my purchase. I'd finger the card, I'd admire the property on the board, I'd rest on my land baron laurels. My friend John, on the other hand, was a shark. No sooner had he scooped up a property than he'd start filling it with houses; three turns later he'd have it covered with hotels. Guess who became the real estate tycoon? Well, the same is true when it comes to advancing your career. Once you land a promotion, you should begin to scout your next one. Take a year or two to master and enjoy the job. But as soon as the job feels comfortable, begin masterminding your *next* advancement.

5. *Trade Marvin Gardens for Atlantic Avenue.* Another friend, Mark, was also a killer at Monopoly: half the time he'd have hotels on Boardwalk and Park Place before I'd even built my first house. But at other times he'd suggest mutually beneficial deals. He'd trade me Ventnor Avenue for Illinois if he was accumulating reds and I was going after

yellows, and somehow even his trading managed to advance his game. Well, the same is true in the workplace. To advance *your* game look for ways to support your co-workers. Become a team player who pitches in; develop a reputation for proposing solutions; and show your bosses that you're familiar with the whole spectrum of jobs in your company.

6. *Give to the Community Chest.* You gave and you got; that's how the Community Chest worked. One turn you'd inherit $100; the next you'd pay school tax of $150. But over the course of the game, both you and the "community" would come out ahead. Well, the same is true at work. You can give your time to a community organization and gain skills that will advance your career. I call it strategic volunteering. How does it work? Say you want to strengthen your skills in accounting before starting your own business. Then volunteer for a nonprofit that needs bookkeeping assistance. Want to get the inside scoop on your customers? Then give time to a church or neighborhood organization that serves people just like them. Want to prove your skills at leadership, or decision making, or handling office politics? Volunteer for the board of a nonprofit where all those qualities are in high demand. And, of course, while you use the experience to build your base of skills, the community gains as well.

7. *Pay in to the Electric Company and Water Works.* When I was a kid I never really got how these utilities worked. I knew you had to fork over cash, but I was never clear on how that turned a profit later. (Mostly, since they required high-level multiplication—the 4s table—my friends and I ignored them.) But the older kids seemed to know, and whenever I played against my brother, he'd buy them up and sting me every time I went around the board. Well, investing in your career is like that. Sometimes you have to fork over money while unsure of the return. It might be for training, or for a trip to see a mentor, or for a library of books and magazines that will build your awareness of your field. When it comes to work, you're your own utility company; that means you've got to pay to keep the energy flowing.

8. *Go to Jail, Go Directly to Jail.* This was the worst! You had to watch your buddies scoot around the board, building hotels and collecting rent, while you sat around and prayed for doubles so you could get free. Arggh! Kind of how it feels sometimes in your career: others scoot past you up the promotions ladder; your department gets sacked while others don't; you make an innocent mistake and watch that good evaluation slip away. And you know it's gonna take more than doubles to fix the situation this time. Well, take heart.

Who said the advancement path is always vertical? It's not. Everyone's career goes sideways at times. It's one of the laws of workplace physics. Your task is to keep your spirits up, to know that *nothing* can set you back permanently (take Donald Trump—please!), and to refocus on your long-range goals. Check in with that mentor. See if your advancement strategy still works. Make adjustments to it if necessary. But don't give up. If you fold early, you'll never win.

Now, as you play Career Monopoly you needn't be cutthroat: it would be dumb to advance yourself at the expense of co-workers or the company. But there's nothing wrong with keeping your personal interests in mind as you go about your daily job. Some of your co-workers are probably doing that right now. Why, they might even have their eyes on the boss's chair! So you better get crackin'. You've already invested in R&D—you've bought this book (which just goes to show that the purchasing department at "You, Inc." is shrewd). Now draw up that strategic plan. Figure out which properties to buy. Find yourself a mentor. Remember: no one's got a monopoly on you but you. And you can take that to the bank.

The Working Wounded Poll

What is the key to getting ahead in your career?

Keeping your nose to the wind (to sniff the latest trends), 23%
Keeping your nose to the grindstone, 36%
Keeping your nose brown, 40%

Poll conducted at *workingwounded.com*

from email to *workingwounded.com*

The Best Way to Get a Promotion . . .

Be on time, learn your job, go the extra mile, and don't suck up to the boss.

from email to *workingwounded.com*

The *Other* Best Way to Get a Promotion . . .

Two words: kiss butt!

"Quit complaining. In these times, most people would be happy to have your job security."

HOW CAN I INCREASE MY CHANCES OF GETTING A PROMOTION?

Dear WW: *I'm watching other people get promoted while I stay in the same old job. I feel like my work is as good as theirs, but somehow I'm just not getting noticed. What am I doing wrong?*

CASPER THE FRIENDLY GHOST

Dear Casper,

Unfortunately there is only one way to guarantee promotion and it's probably beyond your control. That's to pick the right parents—ones with the majority of shares and voting control in a successful family business, who are ready to spend serious time on their golf game in Palm Springs, and who don't think you'll kill the golden goose if you're put in charge. But for us plebes who lack the currency of names like Rockefeller or Gates, the closest thing to a guarantee is to make yourself indispensable. And, unfortunately, a sleeping bag under the desk doesn't cut it anymore: you have to work smarter, not longer.

The following questions have been adapted from *Janice LaRouche's Strategies for Women at Work* (Avon, 1984), which outlines a series of tactics you can use to improve your position and options at work (no matter which bathroom you use):

1. *Can you take the next step in each job or function you perform?* You may occasionally get slapped, but seize every chance to show that you have the interest and potential to contribute more.
2. *Can you solve problems as they arise (instead of passing them on to your boss or co-workers)?* Your boss will appreciate that you're reducing her workload.
3. *Can you find gaps and learn to spot and seize opportunities at work?* In the words of a friend, opportunities rarely come and bite you on the you know what.

4. *Can you do work that others won't do and gain new skills in the process?* Skills is the name of the game. The more you can do, the more valuable you are. But again, you have to create the opportunities for yourself.

5. *Can you create new ways for your company to make money?* Top revenue-generating salespeople often earn more than their bosses. Creating new products, finding new uses for current products and finding new customers are the ticket to more influence and money at work.

Please note that sucking up is not on the list. These are *practical* ways for you to become indispensable. Here's one that worked for me. Years ago, as an intern for a U.S. congresswoman, I offered to do any dumb job that came down the pike. My favorite was delivering letters from the congresswoman to the president. I loved hailing a cab and saying in my best the-nation's-future-could-be-riding-on-this voice, "The White House, please, and hurry." The staff appreciated the fact that I would pitch in wherever needed and rewarded my loyalty with plum assignments.

So the fact that there are people above you on that promotion waiting list doesn't mean your position is immutable. It just means you need to make yourself as seen and valued as they are. I'm forever amazed at how many people think that being invisible is career–enhancing.

from email to *workingwounded.com*

How to Succeed in Business

Sabotage other people's work to make them look bad.
Learn how to forge your boss's signature.

HOW TO SURVIVE YOUR NEXT PERFORMANCE APPRAISAL

Dear WW: *My boss just told me that I've got a performance appraisal coming up next month. I'm not on the best of terms with my boss, so I'm pretty nervous. How can I be sure I get treated fairly?*

WALKING ON EGGSHELLS

Dear Walking,

The business world is divided into two groups—owners and temps. Owners are the ones who make the rules; temps are the ones who have to follow 'em. And unfortunately, one of the rules that owners make is that every temp must be evaluated annually. (If it's any consolation, owners get their evaluations, too; they're just called something else: bank loan reviews, year-end reports, stock prices . . .)

Actually, performance appraisals can be worthwhile: they can give you constructive feedback that will help you grow. But for that to happen—and for you to get treated fairly—the evaluation process must be fair. To make sure yours is, ask the following questions. I've adapted them from *Modern Personnel Checklists* (Warren, Gorham and Lamonte, 1982), that Holy Grail of all things personnel.

1. *Is your boss using clearly defined standards to evaluate you?* Most companies require performance standards that are clear and measurable so that employees aren't subjected solely to their bosses' subjectivity. Before your evaluation, ask (as pleasantly as possible) by what standards you'll be evaluated. *Modern Personnel Checklists* recommends that your supervisor provide you a blank copy of the performance review form at least a week before your review.

2. *Has your performance been adequately observed?* Some bosses observe subordinates on a daily basis; others could barely pick them out of a police lineup. Inquire (gently) as to how and how much you were observed.

3. *Will the evaluation be limited to things that have happened since your last appraisal?* It should be. "Double jeopardy" may work on the game show but it's a losing proposition in the office. Most human resources professionals agree that your boss shouldn't try you twice for the same "crime."

Once the appraisal happens, ask yourself these two additional questions:

1. *Was too much time spent on a few uncharacteristic actions?* Everyone has a bad day. The bulk of your appraisal should focus on your "typical" performance.

2. *Were you rated fairly across the board?* Some evaluators give uniform ratings—all good, all bad, all mediocre—to every aspect of an employee's performance, as if they couldn't take the time to see how the person performed in different aspects of her job. If you think you've been judged unfairly in certain areas, develop a case supporting your performance and take it to personnel. Give them objective measures of your performance—

the quantity produced, the time lines met, the comments you received when the work was turned in and so forth—so they have something other than your boss's subjective appraisal to go on.

You know, performance appraisals are a lot like heading for the coffeepot the morning after a party. The route is a minefield, but if you step carefully, you can claim the reward. I think if you follow this advice and walk carefully across those eggshells, you'll avoid getting scrambled by the process.

from email to *workingwounded.com*

Before That Evaluation, Make Sure You Know What They Expect

From a sign hanging up in my department:

You saw it in the classifieds, but here's what we really meant:

"Flexible hours": work forty hours and get paid for twenty-five

"In our company employees feel valued": those who missed the last round of layoffs, that is

*"No phone calls please": we've filled the job; our
    call for résumés is just a legal formality*
*"Seeking candidates with a wide variety of
    experience": you'll need it to replace the
    three people who just left*
*"Ability to handle a heavy workload": you whine,
    you're fired*

The Working Wounded Toolbox

Now If Only *They* Would Listen . . .
The Skills That Employers Say They're
Looking For

1. The ability to learn
2. The ability to listen and communicate information
3. Innovative problem-solving skills
4. Knowing how to get things done

From the American Society of Training and Development
via *Personal Best* by Joe Tye (Wiley, 1997)

The Working Wounded Quotebook

66 99

A fool who persists in his folly becomes wise.
GEORGE BERNARD SHAW

SHOULD I GO BACK AND GET AN MBA?

Dear WW: *I can't decide if I should go back for my MBA. On one hand I think it will help my career; on the other, it's a lot of time and money.*

STUDYING MY OPTIONS

Dear Studying:

Join the club. At last count (1992–93) there were 372,000 people enrolled in business graduate programs (up almost 40 percent from 1988–89). Even with enrollments leveling off in the mid-1990s, according to my calculations, by the year 2046 there will be more MBAs in the United States than people. And you thought the lawyer glut was scary!

Would the MBA experience be good for you? A qualified yes (but then so are castor oil and enemas). The question is, does the glut of MBAs make the degree meaningless, or is it the price of admission for a management-level job in the future?

Unfortunately, the future value of an MBA is about as predictable as hog bellies on the Chicago exchange with decidedly less short-term gain.

I've seen MBA programs from both sides, as a student and adjunct professor, and I believe that it can pay dividends for you. However, I also think it's important to ask yourself some tough questions before you ante up your time and cash:

1. *Is it worth the money?* Let's do a little cost-benefit analysis (after all, this is *business* school we're talking about). Take the amount of time and money an MBA degree will cost and compare that to other investments you could make in your career—specialized training in your field, nondegree classes, an apprenticeship with a mentor and so on. This kind of comparison is commonly called "opportunity cost analysis" and grasping this concept should allow you to skip approximately the first month of your class in finance.

2. *Is it worth the time?* For most people, there are two concepts that business school conveniently eliminates from your vocabulary—evenings and weekends. Those who plan on working while going to school will lose yet another—sleep. Are you ready for the salt mines?

3. *Is the information you'll be studying current?* There's an old saying in the military that generals are usually trained to fight the last war. MBA programs

can suffer from the same dysfunction. The business world has changed dramatically in the last decade. Has the MBA curriculum at the schools you're considering kept pace? To find out, talk to recent grads (not the ones the school refers you to; ask for the whole list!); check out the reading lists (sure, there are valuable classics, but are *most* of the books the same ones the professors studied when they were students?); ask how they've integrated current topics into the curriculum (such as how to use the Internet and Intranets—and while you're at it, see if they back up their talk with a cutting-edge Web site for their MBA program). And finally look to see if the program gets local business leaders involved in the classroom. The further removed that MBA programs get from the real world the more stale they'll become.

4. *Does an MBA scratch where you itch?* There are lots of reasons to get an MBA—to get ahead, to up your pay, to impress your parents. Before you register, be clear on your goals—and make sure the program and the degree will really help you meet them.

5. *Can you deal with the jokes?* Uh, how many MBAs does it take to screw up a lightbulb company? This is not a degree for the thin-skinned.

Finally, to get a feel for life as an MBA—and a decidedly different point of view from that of university catalogues—check out *Snapshots from Hell: The Making of an MBA* by Peter Robinson (Warner, 1994). It's a revealing peek under the gown of an MBA grad. Not always a pretty sight.

from email to *workingwounded.com*

I Don't Remember Hearing This in Business School

Never mind getting a business degree. The best way to get a raise is to blackmail your boss! Works every time!

Getting a promotion is simple—sleep with the boss. And be good.

The Working Wounded List

What Good Is My MBA if I Can't Talk the Talk? . . . Most Hated Business Buzzwords

1. Downsizing, 39%
2. Reengineering, 32%
3. Empowerment, 15%
4. Paradigm, 14%

5. TQM, 14%
6. Synergy, 14%

Inc. 500 1996 Survey of CEOs

The Working Wounded Quotebook

66 99

A businessman is a hybrid of a dancer and a calculator.

PAUL VALERY

WHAT DOES VOLUNTEERING HAVE TO DO WITH WORK?

Dear WW: *I just started at a law firm where they require all the attorneys to take on a pro bono client. I feel like I've got my hands full with my paying clients. I don't want to pick a fight with my new bosses, but I'm having trouble with this policy.*

IF IT'S MANDATORY, HOW CAN I
BE VOLUNTEERING?

"Sad but true—my career ladder turned out to be a career footstool."

Dear Mandatory,

First, for the benefit of readers who aren't lawyers, let me offer this little instructional quiz:

Pro bono is:
a. Sonny Bono's oldest son;
b. The professional version of amateur bono;
c. What a butcher gives his dog;
d. The practice of providing expertise for free. (The correct answer is "d.")

It's easy to see pro bono work as an encumbrance—work you have to do when you could be billing clients. But the reality is, when it's carefully chosen, pro bono work offers as much to the volunteer as it does to the "voluntee." It should be thought of as "strategic volunteering"—working in an area where you can both give and get.

Here's an example. Several years ago I ran a nonprofit organization. A savvy ad agency took us on as a pro bono client—partially out of the goodness of their hearts, but mostly because our adventurous organization gave them a chance to show more creativity than their regular corporate clients would allow. Three months later we had a slick new promotional campaign—and the agency won a prestigious local advertising award. Their return on this "freebie" far surpassed any "lost" revenue.

Strategic volunteering isn't just for corporations; it works for individuals, too. It can boost your skills (and your sense of accomplishment) in work as well as in "real life." The following questions should help you develop your strategy:

1. *Can you use this as a chance to strengthen your skills?* You may be dynamite when it comes to litigation, but a dud at writing briefs. Pick your weakest area and find a client who needs that kind of help.
2. *Can you use this as a chance to learn more about your clients?* Whether you're a lawyer serving corporate clients or a salesman hawking copier

machines, spending time with your clients is the best way to learn how to serve them. Pick a volunteer gig that puts you where you can learn the most.

3. *What have you always wanted to do?* It's fantasy time! What have you never done because you were too busy earning money? Here's your chance! Indulge.

4. *Do you ever get bored or take your life for granted?* We all tend to narrow our lives to the comfortable and familiar. Nothing wrong with that. But stretching outside that world can generate an exhilarating new perspective. Consider volunteering for a homeless shelter, or for a nonprofit in an ethnic community other than your own. You may never view your life the same way again.

Most workers have to beg their employers for time off to volunteer. Yours are doing you a favor! So go ahead; do the pro bono. It's more fun than the macarena and it'll make Congressman Sonny proud.

from email to *workingwounded.com*

Show Your Boss You're One Smart Cookie

To be honest I think the key to my promotion was that I bought LOTS of Girl Scout cookies from the boss's daughter.

The Working Wounded Quiz

You just handed in your resignation. Under what conditions can your employer force you to stay on the job?

Answer on page 332.

The Working Wounded List

Could The Job Be as Cool as Its Name?

1. Minister of Progress (Aspen Tree Software)
2. Intangible Asset Appraiser (Dow Chemical)

3. Senior Creatologist (Polaroid)
4. Director, Department of the Future
   (TBWA Chiat/Day)
5. Chief Imagination Officer (Gateway 2000)
6. Vice President of Cool (America Online)

from "Job Titles We'd Love to Have," *Fast Company* (premier issue; April/May 1996; June/July 1996; April/May 1997; December/January 1997)

HOW TO SURVIVE THE BUSINESS PRESENTATION BLUES

Dear WW: *My company puts a lot of weight on presentations when they consider promotions, but I hate giving them. I always feel like my work is strong, but that I'll blow it when I present. Any suggestions on how to make a strong presentation?*

STUCK IN PRESENTATION PANIC

Dear Stuck,

For advice on presentations I always turn to that reliable old business primer, the Ten Commandments. It's right there, page 65 (Revised Standard version): *Thou shalt not kill.* Thou shalt not kill with a windy preamble. Thou shalt not kill with too many details. Thou shalt not kill with a serious demeanor and too little levity. It worked for Moses; chances are it will work for you.

Giving a good speech is as easy as counting to two. One: skim a book on speeches at the bookstore or library. Almost any one will do, but *You Are the Message* by Roger Ailes (Currency Press, 1988) is a good choice. This will help get your juices and creativity flowing. Two: ask yourself the following questions:

1. *Who is my audience and what is important to them?* Are they lawyers or salespeople, "suits" or hourly workers, peers or superiors, ready to be convinced of your position or ready to go to war with you? The better you know who you're talking to, the better you can speak to their interests.

2. *What outcome do I hope to get from my presentation?* In sales, the term is "the ask." What are you asking the audience to do or feel? If your presentation doesn't make a point, then what is the point of giving it?

3. *Will my presentation engage my audience's head and heart?* Most people in business have both (although we all know a few who don't). Yet most speakers tend to focus on "just the facts." Fact is, compelling data notwithstanding, most

decisions are made emotionally. So be sure to appeal to both head and heart.

4. *Am I taking my subject too seriously, or not seriously enough?* Jokers and zealots make people uncomfortable in most business settings. Seek a balance in your delivery.

5. *Does my presentation have a beginning, a middle and an end?* Like a good book or movie, your presentation should have an opening that creates interest, a middle that explains your point of view, and a closing with an emotional punch line.

These days it seems like the biggest challenge in giving a presentation is to avoid the dreaded disease "technology for technology's sake." It goes something like this: slides beat talk, videos beat slides, and really fancy computer stuff beats everything else. The irony in this is that the more technology people use, the more we have to turn down the lights. Last week the snoring got so loud in a meeting I attended that I was unable to fall asleep myself. So use technology judiciously. It's no substitute for you.

A little humor goes a long way, too. A few years back, I gave a speech to a group of engineers. I peppered it with jokes, and the audience responded. As I was leaving the stage I passed the next speaker. To my surprise the woman glared at me.

"You aren't supposed to tell jokes here," she muttered under her breath. "It's not your job to entertain. You're just supposed to give a speech." I was speechless. Unfortunately she wasn't.

The Working Wounded Quotebook

If there is a miscommunication, blame yourself not your audience. You are the message.

ROGER AILES

---

from email to *workingwounded.com*

How *Not* to Make a Presentation

I work for the Health Department of our county. A woman came to make a presentation before our board and was clearly very nervous. She wanted to explain how she had been working with the county's eleven small cities and towns, but it came out, "I know I have the support of all our small titties and clowns."

CHAPTER 6

STRUGGLING TO GET OUT

How to Break Out of Your Job and into a New One

MAYBE THERE ARE TIMES YOU *DON'T* WANT TO START AT THE TOP

My dad always warned us that crime doesn't pay. Well, after founding a nonprofit volunteer program called Safety Assistance From the Elderly (S.A.F.E.), I can tell you that crime prevention doesn't pay very well either. But it did teach me something about how to break into a new career.

S.A.F.E. was staffed by senior volunteers who conducted safety checks on the homes of other seniors. One day we got a call from a high-rise senior apartment complex that had experienced a rash of thefts, so I rounded up two of my ace volunteers and we went over to check out the building. Well, it took Ed and Grady all of five minutes to locate the source of the problem. The gardener habitually blocked open a side door while he worked, and since few of the residents locked their apartments, he'd created a burglar's paradise. Ed and Grady congratulated each other on their detective prowess and began to write up their recommendations. As they did, the building's manager tapped me on the shoulder.

"That side door—that's not it," he said. "But I got it figured out. Follow me."

Curious, we followed him to the elevator and up to the top floor of the building. From there we could look down on the broad flat roof of the adjacent building in the complex. "That's the problem," he said triumphantly, pointing at the roof.

"I don't get it," said Grady. "What's the problem?"

The manager squinted at Grady as if he were hopeless. "You don't get it? They use a *helicopter*. If we want to stop them thieves from stealing our things, we gotta keep their helicopters off our roof!"

Well, the idea that a rogue band of burglars was using helicopters to rob seniors of their Social Security checks struck us as pretty remote. But we did give the guy a lot of credit: he was the most creative problem-solver we'd ever met. And he knew a thing or two about burglars. He knew that they rarely enter through the door: they look for a less obvious route in.

Now, that's also a useful thing to realize when it comes to breaking into another job. *You gotta think like a burglar.* You can't expect to enter a new company through the front door. You have to look for less obvious routes that can get you where you want to go.

BREAKING OUT BY BREAKING IN

Unfortunately, most people who are looking for a job think like upstanding citizens. They answer ads in the newspaper, they send résumés, they sit home and pray they'll get picked for an interview. The trouble is, only a fraction of jobs get filled that way, so the upright, front-doorbell-ringing job seeker is left with a horrific case of rejection.

Take Louie, for example. Louie was my office mate a few years back and he wanted out *badly*— so badly, in fact, that while everyone else sipped coffee and soda during meetings, Louie tipped back a bottle of Maalox. (The guy's stomach must have had more acid than all the rain in New York state.) I once asked him why he advertised his problem to the world instead of taking pills, which he could have swallowed surreptitiously. To my surprise he answered, "Ah, I want them to *see* the pain they cause."

"Gee, ever think of getting out?" I wondered.

"You bet. I've sent out fifty résumés."

"How's it going?"

"Terrible! Ten rejection letters, three we'll-get-back-to-you's, two interviews, the rest no answers." His voice turned from angry to defeated. "I think all the jobs go to insiders."

Well, Louie was exactly right. The jobs *do* go to insiders. So the trick is to become an insider yourself. How do you do that? By thinking like a burglar. By finding informants in the company who will give you the inside scoop, and by finding back alleys that lead right to the departments in which you'd like to work. Sound tricky? It's not really. You just need to stop thinking like an honorable, rule-following citizen and start thinking like a crook. Here are some tips to help you "break and enter" into that new job.

HOW TO BURGLE 101

1. *Case the joint.* No self-respecting burglar would break into a building without first having done his homework. He'd know the best time to make an attempt, what he was apt to find and which rooms offered the greatest return. Well, a self-respecting job seeker has homework to do, too.

STRUGGLING TO GET OUT

Before you try to break in, you need to do some digging on your prospective employer.

- You want to learn how the company is organized, which departments might be right for you, and what projects are happening or in the offing.
- You want to learn who the key players are in those departments and who can influence your getting hired.
- And you want to learn as much as you can about the company's business so that when you go for an interview you can impress them with your knowledge.

How do you get all this info? You find informants inside the company.

- First call any contacts you have and ply them for information (this is commonly known as an "information interview"). Then ask them who else to talk to.
- If you have no contacts, call the departments in which you think you might work and talk to the secretaries. Tell them why you're calling and ask them to be your advisors. Secretaries are some of the best-informed people in companies and they're apt to return the compliment with information. Be sure to ask for names of other people to talk to and this

process should land you meetings with people who could influence a hiring decision.

- Call departments in which you *don't* want to work. While they route you to the right departments, you can ask a lot of questions and gather useful data. One of the best jobs I've ever had I got by calling the wrong department.

2. *Check out all the points of entry.* That high-rise manager had the right idea. Few burglars waltz in through the door. They use windows, tunnels, fire escapes, (helicopters?) . . . whatever they can find that will get 'em inside. And that's what you need to do, too. Once you've done your information interviews, you want to use everything you've learned to get yourself considered for a job. Did you learn that the department you want to work in is starting a new project? Call the project manager and tell her why you're essential to her team. Did you learn that someone is about to leave? Call his boss and pitch yourself as his replacement. Don't expect the human resources department to hold the door open and invite you in. That's the *least* dependable way to land a job.

3. *Tailor your break-in to the job.* The best burglars know what tools they'll need and are sure to bring them along. You should do the same. That means bringing *more* than your résumé to your interviews. What to bring? Your meetings with insiders should tell you. It could be possible solu-

tions to a problem you know they're facing: it could be a report you once wrote on a matter related to the prospective job. Or it could be something less tangible. Let me give you an example . . .

When I left S.A.F.E. I interviewed with the chief operating officer of a large health maintenance organization who, an informant had warned me, loved "a show." When the COO barked, "All you've run is a volunteer organization. Where's your management experience?" I kept those words in mind. "Phil," I answered, "you have sixteen people reporting to you. How many would work for you if you couldn't pay them?" He grinned and conceded my management experience. After that I leapt around his office, pointed my finger in his face, and said things that would have made someone in personnel shudder. At one point, using info I'd gathered in my earlier interviews, I noted that the company had a problem with smoking in its hospitals and clinics. "What do you know about smoking?" he challenged. "Nothing," I answered, "but you don't seem to know so much, either." Phil looked me in the eye, broke into a smile and said, "Okay, if you promise to calm down, I'll give you that project to work on."

Now, you don't need to be that outrageous; I was because of my inside information. You just need to tailor your presentation to the person you're meeting—and give him whatever kind of "show" he or she likes.

All of which goes to show that the route to a new job is not always a straight line. Sometimes it's just plain crooked.

The Working Wounded Poll

How truthful are you on your résumé?

It's pure pulp fiction, 5%
I don't exactly lie, but . . . , 41%
Every word is true, 52%

Poll conducted at *workingwounded.com*

from email to *workingwounded.com*

The Straight Poop on How NOT to Get a Job

My absolute worst job interview began after I stepped in a pile of dog poop as I headed out the door for my big appointment at a major Silicon Valley company. I didn't realize at the time that I had actually stepped in it; however, there was an unpleasant smell in the car on the way over. While I was sitting in the posh office of the Silicon Valley executive interviewing me he began to wonder what that gawd-awful smell was. I was a little curious, too, and realized it was on my shoe! At that moment I looked back at the path I had walked and noticed that I had tracked the stuff all the way down the hall and into the man's office! Needless to say, I didn't get the job, and thankfully I didn't get the carpet cleaning bill!

The Working Wounded Quotebook

66 99

It wasn't raining when Noah built the ark.
HOWARD RUFF

HOW TO WRITE A RÉSUMÉ THAT GETS NOTICED

Dear WW: *What do employers look for in a résumé?*
CAUGHT IN RESUMANIA

Dear Resumania,

Like speed bumps, airport metal detectors and portable toilets, résumés are a necessary evil. They're trouble if you take 'em too fast; they have the potential to expose your dirty laundry; and they're all about the process of elimination. But when you're on the move, there's just no way around them. Fortunately, there *are* some ways to make your laundry more presentable and to minimize the chance that you'll be the one eliminated.

The key is packaging (which is not to be confused with distortion). Most people can survive the human resources minefield just by properly packaging what they've actually done. To help you in this effort I offer the following dos and don'ts from a book called *Modern Personnel Checklists* (Warren, Gorham and Lamont, 1982). It's likely that this book, which is a bible for human resource managers, has been well thumbed by the hands that will finger your vitae.

1. *Do's: Does your résumé clearly explain your achievements?* Don't just regurgitate your job description. Talk about the value you've added for your employers. A short list of accomplishments is better than a long list of activities.
2. *Do's: Does your résumé show that you are profit-minded?* Most companies already have enough people who know how to spend money, but are lacking in people who know how to make it or save it. Clearly outline specific examples where your efforts resulted in increased revenues or reduced expenses.
3. *Do's: Does your résumé indicate both stability and a sense of direction?* If not, there are ways you can package your past jobs to give the appearance of both. Try to position your short jobs as rungs on a ladder, emphasizing the common threads between them. This can make it look as if you've left jobs deliberately to seek broader experience. Often it's possible to position your experience

on your résumé to make the interviewer feel that each of your previous jobs has been leading to the one you're currently seeking: that you have been honing your skills and shaping your career so that you can achieve greatness on behalf of the company now hiring.

4. *Do's: Do you use words that match the job description?* These days many companies use computers, programmed to search for key words, to screen résumés. So be sure to make your résumé "computer friendly" or it may never reach those HR fingers.

5. *Don'ts: Does your résumé have long descriptions of your educational history?* There's a reason they call life off campus "the real world."

6. *Don'ts: Does your résumé contain lots of gaps?* Minimize the appearance of gaps by listing your jobs by the year (1990–94, not June 1990 to January 1994). Fill in gaps with volunteer or part-time jobs, which you describe as fully as you do your full-time jobs.

7. *Don'ts: Does your résumé contain lots of trivia?* A hint: your personal section should not be longer than your employment history.

One last tip: become a résumé collector. Sure, it's not as much fun as collecting Red Skelton plates, but it'll be more valuable to your career. Get them from people you respect—co-workers, old bosses, anyone whose résumé has obviously worked—and examine them to see how they became paper heroes. And finally, keep your résumé current. You'll never know when you gotta go—and when you do, you want to be prepared.

The Working Wounded Toolbox

Read This Only *After* You've Written Your Résumé

The amount of time that a human resources manager spends reading most résumés—between thirty seconds and four minutes.

from the *Washington Post* via *The Practical Guide to Practically Everything* by Peter Bernstein (Random House, 1996)

from email to *workingwounded.com*

Sometimes You Wish Your Résumé *Hadn't* Gotten Noticed

I sent in a résumé for a job and was called in for an interview. A few months before the interview I had gotten a "perm" which was growing out and the bangs over my forehead were straight, while the rest of my hair was still fairly curly. So, after my shower in the morning, I used to curl my bangs and hold them in place with Scotch tape, something I had only recently learned to do from a friend. So, that morning I left for the interview, dressed in my best suit and blouse. I met with the interviewer, who was very polite, but never got quite comfortable with me. I just thought we never hit it off . . . which happens. At one point I thought, who cares, this is not working and I got comfortable in my chair, leaning back. Well, the chair fell backward, with me in it. Wearing the narrow skirt I was, I couldn't get up. I was stuck, on my back, in the chair, with both legs waving in the air. I thought I couldn't have felt more stupid. The interviewer helped me up, asking if I was hurt. I thanked him, said I was okay and immediately left. While in the elevator, on the way down from the interview, I noticed my reflection in the shiny metal panel. Well, wrong again, that Scotch tape was still on my forehead, holding those curls in place.

The Working Wounded List

Spin City . . . Most Common Area for Résumé "Embellishment"

1. What you were paid in your last job
2. How long you've spent in a particular job
3. Why you left
4. Your age
5. How far up the ladder you'd really climbed

from Austin★McGregor International
via *Workforce* magazine

THE ART OF THE INFORMATION INTERVIEW

Dear WW: *It's time for me to start job hunting. Unfortunately my job doesn't give me many chances to network. A co-worker suggested I do some information interviews, but that feels so awkward to me. I don't even know where to begin.*

FRIENDS IN ALL THE WRONG PLACES

Dear Friends,

Tango, mambo, limbo, disco—I've danced 'em all. But the trickiest dance of all is the "information interview two-step." You don't have to be a dancin' fool to know that a collision is in the air when both dancers try to lead. And that's usually what happens when "Ms. Inside" is eager to get back to work, and "Mr. Outside" is trying to squeeze out every minute of her time he can.

Information interviews *have* gotten people great jobs, though—and I'm speaking from experience. Sure, I've sent out résumés, too. But they've never produced the same result. When you network, you often hear about jobs *before* they're listed. WARNING: an information interview is not a job interview. The point is to target people who might have ideas about where you should look for a job and to pick their brains and get leads. This is more about engaging your ears than flapping your mouth.

There are lots of books on networking. But as Tom Waits sings, "Fishing for a good time starts with throwing in your line." Troll through your Rolodex and pull out everyone you respect. Hook other contacts from friends, co-workers and family. Don't be shy. The longer your list, the better your chances of reeling in the perfect job. Then, before you pick up the phone, consider the following:

STRUGGLING TO GET OUT

1. *How can I get the person's attention?* Try to get the person on the phone directly, rather than leaving a message. Eight A.M. and 5:30 are the best times to call because the secretary is often not in. My favorite ice-breaker is, "Joe Smith suggested we meet. Do you have thirty minutes in the next six weeks?" Rehearse short answers to the pertinent questions they'll probably ask: Who are you? Why do you want to meet? Why do you think I can help you? Two keys to getting the person to say yes: make her feel flattered by your request, and make her feel that she's calling the shots about the meeting (when to meet, for how long and so forth).

2. *Can you do homework before you meet?* Anyone worth meeting is worth preparing for. You're meeting with this person because you want to pick his brains about a particular company or industry, so check out newspaper articles, annual reports, sales brochures—anything that will give you background and help you frame useful, intelligent questions. You want to prove that you are smart, worth his time and worth giving tips to.

3. *Can you keep it on schedule?* Time is precious, especially when it belongs to someone else. So keep it to the thirty minutes requested. It should go longer only at your host's suggestion.

4. *Can you avoid the hard sell?* This is an "information" interview. Let your host do most of the talking. No pushing or pleading.

5. *Can you remember to say thank you?* Your interviewees are giving you something valuable: their
   time. The least you can do is send a note to thank
   them. Another way to say thanks is to keep them
   posted on the progress you make with the leads
   they gave you, and to let them know when you
   land a job.

No one has better summed up the spirit of the
information interview better than Blanche Dubois,
who said, "I've always depended on the kindness of
strangers." If you follow the tips above, at least one
of the people you meet may not be a stranger for
long.

The Working Wounded Quotebook **" "**

*If we don't change the direction we're going,
we're likely to end up where we're headed.*
ANCIENT CHINESE PROVERB

---

from email to *workingwounded.com*

The Only Thing That Could Be Worse Would Be Getting the Job

The interviewer started by asking me questions: "What kind of gas do you use?" and "What did you eat for breakfast?" He then asked me to laugh, which I thought strange, but did. Next he asked me to do ten push-ups. Finally, he told me that the job had been filled several days before; he just wanted to see how far I'd go for a job.

The Working Wounded List

They Asked You What? . . . Real Questions Asked During Real Job Interviews

- A Wall Street bank asked women MBA graduates, "Would you have an abortion to stay on the fast track?"
- While a discount department store asked interviewees, "How long can you hold your urine?"

Interviewing by Arlene Hirsch (Wiley, 1994)

SHOULD I SIGN A NONDISCLOSURE AGREEMENT TO GET A JOB INTERVIEW?

Dear WW: *Recently I got a recruiting call from a giant software company that I'd kill to work for. But they insist that I sign a nondisclosure agreement before they'll even meet with me. What are the risks of signing?*

TO SIGN OR NOT TO SIGN

Dear Sign:

These days nondisclosure agreements seem to be breeding faster than rabbits. Used to be that only big corporations used them—and selectively at that—to prevent existing employees from leaking trade secrets and customer lists. Now, in a lot of industries, they're virtually standard fare during the interview process because many companies don't want interviewees to divulge any information they received during the interview.

But just because they're standard doesn't mean they're harmless. Judd Lees, an attorney with Williams, Kastner and Gibbs in Bellevue, Washington, believes that most people take these agreements too lightly. They *can* be enforced. More than one overeager soul has been hauled into court by a current or prospective employer for allegedly stealing the company's proprietary information. Some of these people were merely continuing the work they'd been doing *before* talking with the company.

So if blindly signing a nondisclosure agreement is not a good idea, how do you get your foot in the door at the company? Lees recommends the following steps, which would enable you to have your meeting while also protecting who you are and what you know:

1. *Ask to have the agreement mailed to you ahead of time.* Compare their nondisclosure agreement with those in a book of legal forms (available at your local library or law library). Are they throwing you any curveballs versus the standard boilerplate?

2. *Mark your proposed revisions on the agreement and bring it with you to the interview.* Discuss the agreement frankly before beginning any job-related conversation. Ask if the company generally enforces such agreements and in what instances, then note the answers and keep them on file. Should a lawsuit develop, their statements could limit your liability.

3. *Don't assume that your only choices are to sign or not to sign.* Instead ask to modify the agreement to suit your needs. Insist on a time limit: don't sign an agreement in perpetuity. And limit the material covered to confidential information you acquire *after* signing the agreement. Knowledge

you possess *before* signing should be expressly excluded.

4. *If they refuse to accept your changes, think hard.* You need to decide just how badly you want that job—and whether it's worth a lawsuit if they later claim you "misused" their confidential data.

In a nutshell, signing a nondisclosure agreement can be more dangerous than leaving your billfold on a downtown street corner. Lose your billfold and you lose your cash on hand. Sign a nondisclosure agreement that's too broadly written and you might be handing your future to the company, or your bank account to a lawyer.

from email to *workingwounded.com*

And Sometimes the *Company* Discloses Things It Shouldn't

A few years ago I applied for a job, went for an interview and was then asked to return for a second interview because they had narrowed the search to two candidates: me and someone else. Halfway through the second interview I found out that the other candidate was my ex-husband! But it gets even worse. After the second interview the interviewer called me to say they had decided to hire my ex-husband—not because he was more qualified; he wasn't. But because he was a man and would therefore have more responsibilities than I had (because he was sure to be a family's bread-winner). Well, that's what they thought. The truth was that I had custody of our two children and he wasn't paying a penny of their expenses. I was.

from email to *workingwounded.com*

I Guess That Makes Car Delivery the Second Oldest Profession

When I was eighteen, I interviewed for an exciting job listed as "car delivery person," but during the interview I found out they also wanted me to go out to dinner and "be very nice" to the person receiving the car. In other words, this was a new slant on an old profession. Needless to say, I remained at my boring position as a file clerk for two more years!

Working Wounded List

Imagine How I Feel (as a Business Journalist) . . .

Least Respected Professions

1. Union leader
2. Journalist
3. Banker
4. Businessperson

from "Prestige of Professions," *Business Week* (June 9, 1997)

The Working Wounded Quotebook

Be patiently aggressive.

EDSEL FORD

THE IMPORTANCE OF INTERVIEWING THE INTERVIEWER

Dear WW: *I'm going on a lot of job interviews these days. A friend, who just got a great job, told me that he always asks a lot of questions whenever he's interviewing. To me this*

seems pushy, but I'm wondering if by just answering the questions I'm asked, I'm selling myself short?
                              STILL WATERS RUN DEEP

Dear Deep,

You may not believe this, but it's true. I had a friend, an amateur photographer, who was job hunting. He saw an ad for a photo processor and applied. Two minutes into the interview he knew he wasn't their guy. The job required all sorts of arcane knowledge that he didn't have. So he admitted ignorance and, out of sheer curiosity, spent the next twenty minutes grilling the interviewer about photo processing. Well, the very next day (I couldn't make this up) there was an ad in the paper from a different company for the same job. So my friend, armed with all the info he'd learned the day before, interviewed and got the job.

All right, it's a fluke. It'll never happen to you. But it does show the benefit of asking questions. You know, interviews aren't like the dinner table when you were a kid—you don't have to speak only when spoken to. They're your chance to kick the company's tires, to find out if it's a place you really want to work. *National Business Employment Weekly Guide to Interviewing* (Wiley, 1996) says there are three things you need to know before you take a job—and the only way to know them is to turn the tables and start asking questions.

1. *Do you really want the job?* Maybe all you want from a job is a paycheck that's guaranteed to clear. But I bet you'd *also* like an environment and working style that fit your own. If so, asking questions can help you learn the score. Try: Why is this job open? What are the greatest challenges facing this position? What kind of support does this position receive? What's the culture here?

2. *Do you really understand what the company's looking for?* Sure they've given you the basics: the skills, the tasks, the outputs. But what about the more intangible stuff—like temperament or flexibility—that an employer doesn't verbalize? To get a handle on that, ask about the person who had the job before. What kind of person was he or she? What worked? What didn't? Should the job be handled differently this time?

3. *Will you fit in?* Ideally you'll interview with your would-be boss so you can get a sense of that person's style. But even if you don't, ask about the boss's methods: What's the style of supervision? How is performance evaluated? Are employees involved in setting goals and deadlines?

You know the old adage from the theater: the monologue always precedes death? Well, the same is true for interviews. Turning interviews into *dialogues* can keep your job prospects alive.

from email to *workingwounded.com*

This Information Interview Led to a Relationship That Was Short and Sweet

I did an information interview at a company that I thought I really wanted to work at, but while I was talking to the woman she said a number of things that turned me off. By the time I left, I'd decided I didn't want a job there. I'd already asked personnel to send me an application, though, so when it arrived in the mail I decided to have a little fun with it. Next to the question "What office machines can you operate?" I wrote, "Coke and candy." Needless to say I never heard back.

The Working Wounded Quotebook

It's not what we know that hurts us, it's what we think that just ain't so.

SATCHEL PAIGE

The Working Wounded Quiz

Statements made during a job interview are not legally binding on an employer. Employers can only be held accountable for promises made in writing: True or False?

Answer on page 332.

" 'Burned out,' Parker?—I wasn't aware you ever even 'caught fire.' "

WHOSE PERSONNEL FILE IS IT ANYWAY?

Dear WW: *My supervisor is a jerk and I wouldn't put it past her to try to put lies in my personnel file. My*

friends tell me that my file is off limits, but I think that they have to give it to me if I ask. Who is right?
CAN'T JUST FILE IT AWAY

Dear Can't,

Harlequin romances, horoscopes, the stock quotes in the daily paper—whatever is your "must reading," I've got one to add to your list: your personnel file.

Generally your company is required to keep a file with your name, identification number, address, job title, dates of employment, rate of pay, numbers of hours worked each day and each week. But, as you acknowledge in your letter, some don't stop at that. Some supervisors add comments about your performance. And you're right to be concerned—because even if you and your supervisor get along as well as Regis and Kathie Lee, errors can still creep in. And (here's the important part) your personnel file isn't confidential. It can be given to people outside the company. That means that if you apply for another job, your prospective employer has access to the file. For all these reasons you want to know what's in there.

Fortunately, eighteen states have made it relatively easy for you to find out. According to Barbara Repa's *Your Rights in the Workplace* (Nolo Press, 1996) eight states have statutes that allow you to see your file at least once a year (Alaska,

California, Iowa, Louisiana, Maine, Oregon, Pennsylvania and Rhode Island). Another ten states go even further: they allow you to see your file and insert a rebuttal to any mistakes it contains (Connecticut, Delaware, Illinois, Massachusetts, Michigan, Minnesota, Nevada, New Hampshire, Washington and Wisconsin). To actually see and, if necessary, correct your file, take the following steps.

1. *Ask.* If you live in one of the eighteen enlightened states, ask your human resources or personnel department to show you your file. If they refuse, get a copy of the law to show them. (You can get the laws on access to personnel records by calling your local state representative, university law library or legal aid society.) If you live in a state that does not permit you to see your file, ask anyway. They may refuse—but then again, they may not.
2. *Take a look at your state's law.* Even if your employer doesn't refuse, you might want to check out the law because it will tell you if you're permitted to make a copy of your file. You'll probably want to copy it if you find an inaccuracy, or, who knows, maybe just to show your kids.
3. *Correct inaccuracies.* If you find an inaccuracy and you live in one of the states that permits you to

file a correction, do so immediately. If your employer resists, show him the law. If you live in a state that does not permit you to file a correction, ask your employer to let you do so anyway. Present a carefully documented case explaining why the statements are inaccurate—and then hope they're feeling beneficent, because they'll be within their rights if they refuse.

4. *Ask to see your personnel file at former employers.* Believe it or not, some states allow you to see and correct your file up to two years after leaving a job. So if you're concerned about what a former employer may have said, now's the time to check it out. You don't want a surprise from the past to come back and bite you.

Now, I don't want any of this to alarm you. In all likelihood, your personnel file is as pure as the driven snow. But it's a good idea to take precautions, because that department that controls these files is really misnamed. It should be called "only human" resources because, like all the rest of us, they're only human—and sometimes they make mistakes.

from email to *workingwounded.com*

Guess Who Flunked the Morality Test?

I went to interview to work in a clothing store. After talking to me for a few minutes, the owner sent me to a back room, which was hot and tiny, and filled with boxes and trash, to fill out a "morality" test. I finished the test and tried to return to the main part of the store, but the door was locked. The woman had locked me in! I banged on the door and called to her but she didn't come. I could hear that she was busy with customers so I waited awhile, then banged again. She finally came for me an hour later, all apologetic, saying she had forgotten about me. She gave me the job, but I wouldn't take it!

" "

The Working Wounded Quotebook

To change one's life: start immediately, do it flamboyantly—no exceptions.

WILLIAM JAMES

CHAPTER 7

PUSHED TO PERFORM

How to Succeed in Sales
(Even if You're Not in Sales)

HOW I LEARNED FROM A PRO (OR, GETTING A WHIFF OF SALES)

Say "sales" and most people picture a fast-talking guy wearing pinky rings and a polyester suit, right? Well, there's just one problem with that picture: *you're* not in it (unless, of course, you're like me, from New Jersey, where lots of people still dress that way).

"Hey, wait a minute," you say, "I'm not in sales, why should I be in that picture?" "Because," I respond, "you don't have to be in 'sales' to do a lot of selling." If you're in business you're selling whether you call it that or not. Ever tried to swap a day off with a co-worker, for instance? Ever try to get your boss to give you a raise? Ever try to get someone in another department to bend the rules for one of your special projects? Might as well add selling to your business card 'cause the folks down at the used-car lot don't have anything on you.

And speaking of used-car lots—that's where I learned most of what I know. My dad owned a Chevy dealership and the lot was like a university where I got a Bachelor of Science in sales. And what a glorious BS it was! Through the years I learned from every member of the faculty, but Harry was my favorite. Harry knew that most people bought cars after visiting several dealers, and that eventually the salesmen became an indistinguishable blur. So he wanted to distinguish himself. He believed that if he stood out from the rest, customers would remember—and buy from—him. Well, Harry distinguished himself all right. He would sit down with customers in his office and, while meticulously weighing the merits of a Chevy versus an Olds, take off his shoe. Then, as if it were the most ordinary thing in the world, he would jam his nose inside, take a big whiff, and carefully place the shoe on his desk. It would remain there for the duration of his pitch. Crazy? You bet. But it worked. He was memorable all right and he was my father's top grossing salesman for years.

Now, I would hardly suggest you follow Harry's example. (Another salesman did and almost asphyxiated himself. Apparently Harry was the only one who could pull that off *and* close the sale.) But there are countless other real-world professors out there from whom, if you pay close attention, you can learn an MBA's worth about sales.

LIFE'S OTHER SURE THING (HINT, IT ALSO HAS FIVE LETTERS)

Watch a waiter, for example, talk a reluctant diner into a calorie-laden dessert. Or eavesdrop on two teenage girls in a dressing room when one is convincing the other to buy (yet another) pair of jeans. Notice what words they use to push the buyer over the edge. Notice when they *stop* talking to give the buyer room to convince herself. Notice the appeals to emotion over intellect, the way they seem to read the buyer's concerns. But don't just watch as an outside observer. Put yourself *inside* the "customers'" heads. What's going on in there? What emotional strings have the sellers pulled to move them from no to yes? These situations are no different from sales situations you encounter at work—whether you're selling a proposal to your boss or a widget to a customer. Sales is sales is sales. And you're not being paranoid to believe it's everywhere.

Selling is so ubiquitous, in fact, that it belongs

right up there on that list of life's sure things along-side death and taxes. Unfortunately, for many people, selling (or dealing with a salesperson) is as mortifying as those other two. So I've developed a little primer, modeled after a well-known tome— no, not *Death of a Salesman!*—*On Death and Dying* by Elisabeth Kübler-Ross (Macmillan, 1969). I call it The Five Stages of Sales and Selling.

THE FIVE STAGES OF SALES AND SELLING

- Stage One: *Denial*—Ever go into a department, computer or jewelry store sure you were only going to window-shop? Yep, that's where most commissions are earned: from customers in heavy denial about their need to make a purchase. That's why I always laugh when I hear the saying "the customer is always right." If the customer were always right, most wouldn't be customers in the first place! So how do you deal with a customer in deep denial? Whether it's co-workers who won't buy your idea, or prospects considering your product, get 'em talking. Given the right prompts, most people will tell you exactly what you need to know to persuade them. They'll tell you what stands in the way of their buying. They'll reveal their emotional hooks. They'll demonstrate, through their own style of talking and asking questions, an effective way to approach them. You've just got to be patient enough to listen and learn.

They may also give you a sense of just how entrenched their denial is. That's an important thing to determine because some people, unfortunately, never get past this stage. If you sense the denial is permanent cut bait! Save your energy for the next prospect.

- Stage Two: *Anger*—This is what happens when the customer finds out that the price *you* have in mind is not exactly what *he* had in mind. The technical term is "objections." But don't retreat! Anger is a predictable, unavoidable phase of the sales process, and one that the customer will pass through if you play your cards correctly. So whether it's a committee that's objecting to your proposal, or a client who's objecting to the delivery date you've offered, first listen carefully and calmly to each objection; make the customer feel heard. Then answer each objection as thoroughly as possible. *Tailor your answers to the customer* using everything you learned in the previous stage.

Don't be fooled by forceful, angry objections. Customers are like five-year-old boys: they show their interest by hitting—hitting you with every arcane objection they can muster. Just answer these objections diligently—and with the breezy confidence that the sale is just around the corner.

- Stage Three: *Bargaining*—Ah, the light at the end of the tunnel. You know you're closing in on a sale when they start negotiating over terms. Unfortunately, that's also where a lot of sales get lost. To keep your sale on track—whether you're selling your boss on a raise or a customer on an Airstream—keep the following pointers in mind. First: continue to remind her about why she wants the "product" while you negotiate the terms. Sales get lost when the bargaining is isolated to facts and figures and gets too removed from what brought you together in the first place. Second: forget what you've heard about driving a hard bargain. The goal is not to clean out the buyer's pockets. It's to make a respectable sale this time *and* create a loyal customer for the future.

- Stage Four: *Depression*—This is what hits the customer as he realizes he's close to signing the deal—and it's a precarious moment for the seller because in that moment, the customer often comes dangerously close to reneging. It takes skill, patience and a high threshold for anxiety to walk the buyer through this stage. First: listen. Let him talk out his mixed feelings. If you try to paper over them with the benefits of your deal he's liable to distrust you and walk out. Second: if he utters those blood-chilling words, "Let me sleep on it," resist the temptation to kick into hard sell. More sales are lost by forcing a customer's hand than by letting him assure himself he's doing the right thing. So give him a little time *while scheduling a follow-up conversation*. The goal is to give him some line—not to let him off the hook.

- Stage Five: *Acceptance*—Finally. The customer accepts the fact that he's going to buy. Bring out the champagne! Unless, of course, you've forgotten to "close" the deal. And hard as it is to believe, there *are* sellers who do. They walk the customer through the first four stages, right to the point where she says she needs a little more time to think, and then fail to bring her back. Perhaps these sellers fear rejection. Perhaps they question their ability to turn a "depressed" or wavering customer around. For whatever reason, instead of granting a limited time to "sleep on" the decision, they let the sale slumber into death.

How to avoid this pitfall? Simply follow up. Stay on the sleeper's case. Call her (repeatedly, if necessary). Schedule a meeting to continue the discussion. Keep communication open until she buys or sends you away. You've done the hard work already. Gentle massaging should be all you need to turn it into a sale.

These are the five stages of sales and selling. Hopefully, the techniques we've presented for coping with each stage will make your sales experience a little less taxing, and a lot less deadly.

The Working Wounded Poll

When you're trying to make a sale, how do you deal with the "gatekeeper" between you and the person you need to meet?

Try to go over 'em, 20%
Try to go around 'em, 36%
Try to deal directly with 'em, 44%

Poll conducted at workingwounded.com

from email to *workingwounded.com*

Is This What They Mean When They Talk About Nailing the Sale?

My very first sales job was in a store that sold recliners. The store used classic "bait and switch" tactics. We advertised a chair that cost $39, but as *soon as a customer came to see it we were supposed to lead him to chairs that cost much more. In fact, we had only one of the $39 chairs, and it was literally nailed to the floor. The store's owner wanted to make sure that no sales person ever sold it. He threatened to fire us if we ever even tried. I wonder sometimes why that job didn't dissuade me from a career in sales.*

The Working Wounded Quotebook

" "

Remember the 10-3-1 rule. Ten calls lead to three presentations which results in one sale. We need people who won't shrink from that kind of rejection.

DENNIS TAMCSIN

DO I HAVE WHAT IT TAKES TO MAKE IT IN SALES?

Dear WW: *I've been doing technical support for my company and have a good relationship with a number of accounts. My boss now wants me to help with sales and*

I said yes. I'm no fool—I want to keep my job. But I'm a techie and don't know the first thing about selling.

HELP!

Dear Help,

I always like to get input from experts before I answer letters, so I called several people who run sales seminars and asked them to tell me the one skill that's essential for success in sales. Remarkably, they were unanimous in their opinions: the key to being a successful sales person is to be a graduate of an expensive sales seminar.

Well, let me spare you the tuition. You already have something far more important than what you'd learn in a seminar: a working relationship with potential customers. You want to tread carefully on those relationships (there's nothing like a clumsy sales pitch to sour a relationship) but if you can continue to think of yourself as *solving their problems,* you'll be on the road to sales success. The following questions should help. They've been adapted from *You Can't Teach a Kid to Ride a Bike at a Seminar* by David Sandler (Dutton, 1995).

1. *Who's most likely to buy your product or service?* The sales term is "prospecting." Before you make a pitch, you need to take the pulse of your contacts to see if the time and conditions are right for a sale.

2. *What is your prospect's pain?* People don't buy to answer a need; they buy to assuage a pain. It may be a big pain—things that take too long or cost too much done the current way; or it may be a small pain—a minor inconvenience that causes them to groan each time they face a certain task. Either way, your job is to locate their discomfort. But since most people won't volunteer it, you'll have to draw it out. As the saying goes, a salesperson's most important tool is his ears.

3. *Can you assuage the pain?* Forget about selling your product. Sell a solution to your prospect's pain.

4. *Does your prospect have a budget?* If not, save your breath and find another one who does. If all you can come up with are the budget-challenged, see if those people know other cookie jars they can raid.

5. *Can your prospect make the decision?* Even the budget-surplused often need input before they make a decision. So try to get all the decision-influencers to hear your pitch at the same time. It sure beats repeating yourself again and again and again and . . .

I can see why, as a techie, you feel uncertain about switching to sales. But consider this: Albert Einstein, the ultimate techie, once said, "If I had my life to live over again, I would elect to be a trader of goods rather than a student of science." Well, Help, here's your chance. Do it for Al.

The Working Wounded Quotebook **" "**

In our factory we make lipstick, in our ads we sell hope.

CHARLES REVLON

---

from email to *workingwounded.com*

When the Sales Life Just Doesn't Cut It

I've always heard that people make a lot of money in sales. Well, one day a friend gave me a clipping she found in the newspaper for a company that was looking for sales representatives to sell cutlery, working out of their homes. I thought I'd give it a try. I went to a training session and they told us that the commission was 12% for every sale. The knives looked pretty good and I figured I could sell enough to make some decent money, so I signed up. Well, first I had to buy a set of all the knives for

> *my demonstrations. That cost $350. Then, I worked for weeks setting up sales calls ("kitchen parties" we were supposed to call them). I must have done fifteen kitchen parties in the first three months I had the job and the only people who actually bought any of the stuff were my relatives. By the time I decided to quit I'd made $28.30 in commissions. Whoopee. (And I don't even like the knives.)*

HOW TO TEST YOUR ASSUMPTIONS SO THEY DON'T TEST YOU

Dear WW: *My company requires that each salesperson develop projections for the coming year. I have a new boss and she ripped my forecast saying my assumptions were too rosy. But I based them on sales from last year, so they should be accurate.*

IT'S SAFE TO ASSUME I'VE GOT A PROBLEM

Dear Safe,

If you went sailing you would never assume the wind, weather, tides and traffic would be the same as they were on a prior year's sail. Yet in business we

"Fine, Al, and how are you, your charming wife, Joni; your two wonderful children, Charles and Lisa, ages thirteen and fifteen; and your delightful German short-haired pointer, Avondale?"

often leap to the conclusion that next year's conditions will be a replay of last year's. Can you say "Exxon *Valdez*"?

Unfortunately, few things are as dangerous to a business as faulty assumptions—because they are to a business what a compass is to sailors. They orient you to your ultimate port-o'-call as well as through the shifting waters you navigate daily. And assumptions are especially difficult because, for most of us, they are so hard to get a handle on.

It sounds like your boss has fired a shot across your bow. You should grab this chance to reevaluate the seaworthiness of your thinking. The following questions may help you do so. They've been adapted from *Asking "Just Right" Business Questions* by Curtis Page and Charles Seldon (Empower Press, 1994).

1. *Just what* are *your assumptions?* Welcome to the business version of "It's a Wonderful Life." For the next several hours you need to examine your company and marketplace from the outside. You need to look at everything that has an impact on your sales: your customers, your competitors, your *potential* competitors, the economy . . . Even look at your co-workers because they can influence how well your company delivers on your promises. Write down everything you know about those elements that can affect your sales.

2. *When was the last time you tested your assumptions?* Now that you've ballparked your assumptions, it's time to put them to the test. Seek external proof (that is, from a source outside your brain) that what you believe is true. Use the library, trade journals, market research, and other resources to correct or fine-tune your thinking. One manager I know tried to visit a competitor every week. Have you made a weekly commitment to stay on top of your assumptions?

3. *Consider the consequences: what if you're wrong? And if you're wrong, would you suffer a surface wound or a fatal blow?* Microsoft acknowledged that it had

mistakenly assumed that people would want to collect computer CDs just as they do music CDs. Now they realize that people are more interested in surfing the endless Internet than owning a finite amount of content. The company shifted direction and redoubled its commitment to the Net. A deep-pocketed behemoth like Microsoft can survive this kind of misassumption. Can you?

And since we're on the subject of assumptions, let me point out one more. Never assume you know what your boss is talking about. Pin her down. Find out her specific concerns. It's better to look dumb momentarily as you learn to be smart than to risk running into that same reef over and over again. Happy sailing!

from email to *workingwounded.com*

What? You Assumed You Could *Buy* Something Here?

I called a hair salon to find out how late they were open—I needed to drop by and get some shampoo. They said 5:00, so I made a point of leaving work a bit early so I could be there before they closed. I got there about 4:50, selected the product, and placed it on the counter. The lady behind the counter refused to sell it to me because they had closed the register. I indicated that they were still open for another ten minutes and asked again that she ring it up. Again, she said the register is closed out and that she couldn't sell it to me. I told her I had called to verify that they'd be open, and left work early for that reason. She said, "Oh, we are still open." I pointed out the fact that they were refusing my business, and by my reckoning that meant they were closed. Again, she said they were open, but couldn't name a product or service that they could sell me. After a full ten minutes of going around like this, I got her name and left the store. The next day I called her supervisor and explained what happened. She told me that it was standard policy to close the registers at fifteen minutes before closing and that her employee had acted as she was instructed to. She then went on to insist that I should not have "cut it so close" as to come in ten minutes before closing and expect them to sell me something. I assured her that I would never expect them to sell me anything ever again.

The Working Wounded List

Where Does All The Time Go? . . . A Day in the Life of a Salesperson

1. Meetings
2. Training
3. Actually selling

from Ron Volper Group via Anne Fisher, "Willy Loman Couldn't Cut It" (*Fortune*, November 11, 1996)

The Working Wounded Toolbox

Common Sense Doesn't Always Sell . . . Counterintuitive Notions About Sales

- If you don't lose 20 percent of your sales on price your prices aren't high enough
- You can't confer a benefit on an unwilling recipient
- Competitors are friends in disguise
- The shocker, "I am the problem."

from *Flight of the Buffalo* by James Belaser and Ralph Stayer (Warner, 1994)

HOW TO NEGOTIATE A
HIGH-STAKES SALE

Dear WW: *My boss just asked me to negotiate a big contract on behalf of my company. I've never negotiated anything for such high stakes before. What can I do to prepare?*

READY TO GO FOR THE JUGULAR

Dear Jugular,

You know how everything has a slogan these days? "Be all you can be." "Where do you want to go today?" "Ten percent real fruit juice." Well, with all this sloganeering, it suddenly dawned on me that capitalism, the system that pumps the hot air into all those slogans, is, itself, slogan-free. So to fill this egregious void, I developed three slogans and tested them scientifically on a downtown street corner. "Capitalism: Show Me the Money" was my favorite, but turned out to be already licensed by Hollywood. "Capitalism: Even the Russkies Are Doing It!" had a certain ring. But the winner in a landslide was "Capitalism—Get All You Can!"

Now, what does this have to do with negotiating? Everything. Most people believe that the goal in negotiation is to get all you can—to vanquish the "opponent" as if you were at war. But negotiation isn't war. It's trying to reach an agreement. And the goal should always be to make both sides come out winners—because that way you can continue to work together smoothly.

So as you prepare for your big negotiation ask yourself the following questions. I've adapted them from a book called *Roger Dawson's Secrets of Power Negotiating* (Career Press, 1995).

1. *Are you assuming that the party across the table wants the same thing you do?* My sister liked green M&Ms and I liked red ones. The beauty of life is that sometimes you can get exactly what you want because the other party's interests lie elsewhere. Take the time to dig beneath the surface to find out what they really want—And if you try sometimes—you just may find, you'll get what you need. (From what I'm told Mick Jagger and the Rolling Stones swear by this approach.)

2. *Can you get what you want by sweetening the deal for the other party?* My brother's taste in M&Ms was less easily solved: like me, he loved the reds. But he also hated browns. So one day I offered a "package deal." I said I'd take all the browns off his hands if we could split the reds. That was our last fight over M&Ms. It gave me terrific insight about how to overcome resistance in business negotiations. And gave my dentist a house in the country.

3. *Can you leave something on the table?* Joseph Kennedy, Sr., observed, "Only fools go for the

last dollar." You know why? Because most negotiations mark the *beginning* of a relationship, not
the end—and it's tough to develop a positive
relationship with someone who feels taken
advantage of.

Now don't get me wrong. I'm not advocating
that you negotiate from a position of weakness. You
need to know your interests and be sure they get
met. But this is a business negotiation not a bar
fight, and the most successful negotiations are col-
laborative rather than adversarial. Remember, in
the words of an English proverb, "A lean compromise is better than a fat lawsuit."

The Working Wounded Quotebook

66 99

*Don't ever assume that the other fellow has
intelligence to match yours. He may have
more.*

TERRY THOMAS

from email to *workingwounded.com*

Who Says We Don't Give Salesmen Enough Credit?

I was in an appliance store and I overheard a sales-man trying to calm down a customer who was upset because his credit had to be reviewed before he could make a purchase. The customer yelled at the poor salesman, "Do you know where you can stick your credit card?" The salesman calmly responded, "I'm very sorry, sir, but there's already a washer and dryer up there."

The Working Wounded Toolbox

The Cause of Death (of a Salesman's Pitch) . . . Common Reasons Why Sales Are Lost

1. Wrong seller
2. Wrong product
3. Wrong price
4. Wrong time
5. Wrong sales technique
6. Never asked for the sale

from *Relationship Selling* by Jim Cathcart (Perigree, 1990)

HOW TO GET OUT OF A SALES SLUMP

Dear WW: *I've always been one of the best salespeople in my company. But this year, I'm stuck in the middle of the pack. Any ideas for how to get out of a slump?*
THE SMILE AND THE SHOESHINE
AIN'T WORKING

Dear Ain't Working,

Years ago I was walking down a street in Manhattan when a panhandler came ambling toward me. I was about to walk around him when he suddenly reached into his coat and pulled out a telephone. He put the receiver to his ear, talked animatedly for a moment, then handed the receiver to me. "It's Norway," he said, "for you." I laughed long and loud, told him to take a message, then handed the guy a five.

I'm sure I wasn't his first sale of the day—nor his last. It was because he managed to hold on to the three things it takes to stay on top in sales: attitude, opportunities and technique. His attitude was confident (he *knew* he was going to blow me away). He created opportunities where none existed (after all, I was about to walk away). And his technique was brilliant (a telephone call from *Norway?*).

To see how you stack up in those three areas, try asking yourself the following questions. They're adapted from a book called *Relationship Selling: The Key to Getting and Keeping Customers* by Jim Cathcart (Perigree, 1990).

1. *How's your attitude? Have you lost confidence in yourself or your product?* Nothing saps confidence like sagging sales, but customers smell blood in the water faster than sharks. So find ways to trick yourself into projecting confidence even when you're down. Letters from satisfied customers might help; so might developing hobbies away from work. Success off the job can be infectious.

2. *Are you creating opportunities? Or are you coasting?* When sales are strong it's easy to let prospecting slide. Sounds like it might be time to burn some shoe leather. Are there groups of potential customers you haven't tapped? Competitors' customers you can hit? Think back to what you did in the early days and see if your own prospecting savvy can save you.

3. *How's your technique? Have you become too creative—or not creative enough?* It's easy, when you've been at it for a while, to offer the same old pitch to everyone. Stop giving the same generic sales pitch and start adapting your pitch to the specific problems of specific customers. If you're not solving their problems you're wasting their time.

It's also a good idea to check in regularly with the people who have spurned you. Talking to your "rejects" might not seem conducive to boosting your spirits *or* your sales—but who can better tell you what went wrong?

Everyone gets a wake-up call from time to time and it sounds like this is yours. But if you rededicate yourself to doing the little things that got you to the top in the first place, you'll head off those scarier calls from Norway.

The Working Wounded List

Thrown for a Loss . . . For Every $100 Million of Sales, There Are . . .

- 1,365 bad checks
- 229 shoplifting apprehensions
- 68 switched price tags
- 55 credit card scams
- 28 employee theft apprehensions

from University of Florida Security Research Project via "Retailers and Crime," *World Business* (March/April 1996)

from email to *workingwounded.com*

This Could Trigger a Sales Slump

If our customers only knew that our product is made from recycled socks . . .

The Working Wounded Quiz

?

You are a full-time salesperson who is paid totally by commissions. If your commissions fall to zero, would your employer still have to pay you the minimum wage for the time you worked?

Answer on page 332.

THE GOOD NEWS ABOUT CUSTOMER COMPLAINTS

Dear WW: *Recently my boss's cousin was shopping in our store. One of my sales clerks screwed up while waiting on her, and then got rude when the mistake was pointed out. Hell hath no fury like a boss with an annoyed relative, and he's taking it out on me. What can I do?*

CURSE OF THE COMPLAINING COUSIN

Dear Curse,

My five-year-old daughter has a new favorite game. It's called opposite day. On opposite day everything is backward: you say good night when

199

you wake up; *parents* have to say please; and everyone eats dessert first!

Well, I think your boss could profit from playing opposite day because he doesn't recognize that when it comes to customer feedback, bad news can be good. It's your very own down-in-the-trenches, indisputable, totally free market research. Customers who take the trouble to complain are teaching you how to do your business better. They're also, often, the most *invested* customers you have, the ones who need or want your product or service the most. Responding to their complaints can often turn them into proselytizing lifetime loyalists.

The following questions, adapted from *A Complaint Is a Gift* by Janelle Barlow and Claus Moller (Berrett-Koehler, 1996), can help your company maximize its learning from customer complaints:

1. *Are employees encouraged to convey all customer complaints to management?* Most companies have refined the art of killing the messenger, which means employees stop bringing complaints to management. As a result, the company never gets to learn from its mistakes.
2. *Do you make it easy for customers to complain?* Recently I offered "constructive criticism" to a clerk at a department store. He told me I could

either wait until the manager returned ("But I have to warn you, it could be anywhere between ten minutes and three hours") or I could call a long-distance number at company headquarters ("No, I can't let you call from here"). I respectfully declined the opportunity to compete in their customer complaint obstacle course. A valuable learning opportunity for them, gone.

3. *Is there a process for following up on complaints?* There's no surer way to lose a customer than to ignore his or her complaint. And no better way to secure a customer than to show him or her you've listened.

4. *Do you learn from your complaints?* I recently returned a chair to my local hardware store, only to hear: "You know, we've gotten almost every one of those back. They're the worst product we've ever carried!" Minutes later I passed stacks of the same chair on a prominent end display . . .

Now, it's never easy to be in the line of a customer's ire. But it sure beats the alternative—having the angry shopper vent her frustration on ten potential customers. So call your boss's cousin back. Show her you're truly sorry about what happened; enumerate the steps you've taken to make sure it doesn't happen again. And show your boss you've won back his cousin's business (and hopefully her affections). For that is the best opposite day feat of all: taking a customer whose business is out the door and turning her into a customer for life.

The Working Wounded Quotebook

66 99

Profits come from customers, not products.
TOM JOHNSON

---

from email to *workingwounded.com*

Talk About Not Connecting with the Customer . . .

I overheard a customer service rep at the airport talking to a couple who were complaining because they had just missed their connecting flight. Very tactfully she tried to explain their problem: "People think the Denver International Airport is an international airport but it's just not." The couple was trying to complete their flight to Tulsa, Oklahoma. Last I checked, that was still in the United States.

Two shoe salesmen find themselves in a remote part of Africa. One contacts his office, "No prospect of sales, natives don't wear shoes." The second says, "No one wears shoes, we can dominate market. Send all possible stock."

AKIO MORITA

CHAPTER 8

STAYING ALIVE

How to Make Work Less Dangerous to Your Health

GIVE ME A BRAKE

When I was a kid my mother used to say she couldn't wait for me to grow up and get a job. Not because she wanted me out of the house, but because by then, she figured, I'd stop being a danger to myself. I'd stop constantly risking life and limb in "foolish" teenage amusements. But what was she talking about? How could she possibly think that playing chicken on a one-lane bridge was more perilous than arguing with a supervisor? Or that jumping from the roof of the garage to get the attention of a girl was more harmful than pulling consecutive all-nighters to get a proposal in the mail? Or that downing a dozen Whoppers with as many Cokes and fries was more artery-clogging than the food in the average workplace cafeteria? Why, work is far more dangerous than any of the crazy games I played as a teen! In fact, if anything, those games *prepared* me for the world of work. One of them actually taught me something that has helped to keep me healthy . . .

When I was in high school we often played a game called "cat and mouse." It was simple. We'd hop into our cars and race around the neighborhood trying to catch each other. Some played it as a game of short-cuts and anticipation: they'd try to get inside the other driver's head to guess where he was going. Others just tried to get inside the other driver's trunk. My friends Danny and John were among the latter.

One night I was riding in the "mouse" car with Danny while John rode in our dust at about forty miles an hour. (John and Danny were the Beavis and Butt-head of cat and mouse: they didn't *play* the game, they *lived* it.) As we raced through our suburban neighborhood I turned to Danny and observed, "You know, Danny, my sister was rear-ended last week. According to the cops, whenever you get hit from behind it's almost always the other driver's fault."

No sooner were the words out of my mouth, than Danny flashed me a grin, raised his knee to his chest and slammed his foot on the brake. (Later he described that moment as orgasmic: he'd had a vision of the car he would buy with his insurance settlement from John.) But John was a pro. He swerved sharply to the right, careened across three front yards, and stopped deftly, inches from a wooden fence. I bet even the engineers at Dodge had no idea that a six-year-old Duster possessed such off-road maneuverability.

Now, what does this story have to do with health and the workplace? More than the fact that I've lived to tell it! When it comes to staying healthy at work, most of us are like John and Danny—followers. Instead of following a '64 Comet or a dumb suggestion from a friend, we follow our company's health policies, insurance mandates and doctors' orders. And, like John and Danny, we rarely think about the consequences of our actions.

THE MAN WITH X-RAY VISION

Now, I can hear you saying: "What's the problem? Doctors and insurance companies are pros when it comes to health." Well, I agree: they're pros at maintaining the health of their bottom line! And that's the problem. What the company, the doctor and the insurance company recommend may *not* be in your best interest.

Don't believe me? Check this out. For several years my wife and I were sold on Dr. Mike: above all, we liked his willingness to answer all our questions.

Only one thing had us bothered: he investigated almost every ailment with an X ray. Well, three years into our relationship with him I did some consulting for our health insurer and guess what I discovered? Mike owned his X-ray machine and had turned it into a profit center for his practice! Now, I'm sure we needed *some* of those X rays—but I bet we didn't need them all. And in addition to being unnecessary, they were expensive, and not entirely benign. That was a useful lesson in how my needs and my doctor's don't always coincide.

The moral of this story is: if you want the best health care, you need to give up the follower role and take the lead. You need to ask a lot of questions, you need to demand the services you feel you need, you need to act like you're in charge. In short, *you* need to be the manager of your own "managed care." There are four areas in which you need to do this: with the insurance company, on the job, in the doctor's office and at home. We'll take them one at a time.

TO PARAPHRASE WOODY ALLEN, HELL IS PROBABLY FULL OF INSURANCE SALESMEN

1. *Insure that you get what you want from your insurer.*
   Not all insurance is created equal. That's the first

thing you need to know. Some plans offer better coverage than others when it comes to *your family's* needs. So if you're lucky enough to work for a company that still offers a choice, do your homework.

- Read the fine print to compare the coverage offered by different plans. Based on your medical history, pick the one that offers the best coverage of what you're likely to need.
- Compare the procedures for challenging insurance company decisions. Some make it easier to challenge a rejected claim.
- Talk to other people who have used those plans and see how they feel about the coverage. You can even call your state insurance commissioner to compare the records of different companies.
- Talk to the people in personnel. Ask which plan they've chosen for their personal coverage and why.

If you're not among the anointed (that is, those who work for a company that offers an insurance choice) you're probably being pushed into some form of managed care. You know why, don't you? Because it's cheaper—cheaper for your employer, cheaper for the insurance company and possibly cheaper for you. So what's the catch? (You're smart to ask.) Part of what makes it cheaper is that they make it harder for you to get care. You have to go through a "primary care physician" to get access to a specialist, and it's not a gate they open easily. Now, that doesn't mean that managed care is bad—it's not. According to studies, patient care is just as good in most managed care plans as it is in most fee-for-service situations. But it does require you to be assertive.

- Push to see a specialist when you feel it's necessary. Don't take no for an answer.
- Push to get your procedures scheduled quickly. Don't believe that the "first opening" is really three weeks later.
- Ask for an "emergency slot" when scheduling if you feel your appointment can't wait.

ARE YOU ALLERGIC TO YOUR JOB?

2. *Punch the clock without it punching you back.* Now, certainly I'm not the first to point out that while your everlovin' company is kind enough to provide you with health insurance, it's often one of the primary reasons you get sick in the first place. From the stress you feel about keeping up, to the

recirculated air you breathe every day, the workplace is full of potential hazards. Fortunately, there
are things you can do to change that. From EPA
(Environmental Protection Agency) regulations
to the Americans with Disabilities Act, the law
books are filled with laws and statutes that protect
workers' rights to a safe and healthy work environment. So if you feel your workplace is
unhealthy:

• Talk to your boss, talk to the folks in human
  resources, get other employees to talk to them,
  too.
• Bring them medical studies that support your
  argument, or mention regulations you feel
  they're violating. (Your local librarian, law
  school or bar association can help you.)
• Consider filing an official complaint with your
  union (if you're one of those people who
  doesn't automatically think that AFL stands for
  the American Football League), the EPA,
  OSHA (Occupational Safety and Health
  Administration) or their state equivalents.
  (Some regulations even allow complaints to be
  filed anonymously.)

  Meanwhile, take the lead in reducing hazards
in the areas you *can* control.

• Reduce your stress with regular exercise.
  Meditation is helpful (in Jersey we used to call

'em naps); so is keeping a journal and visiting the award-winnings *http://workingwounded.com.*

- Prevent repetitive strain injuries by changing your working position and taking breaks.
- Stop eating the mystery meat in the cafeteria; go for the mystery salad.

QUESTION AUTHORITY

3. *Treat your doctor with a lot of questions.* Someone once gave me a great tip on how to lower my anxiety when meeting with an intimidating person: imagine the person with a string of red licorice dangling from her mouth. It works every time! Well, I recommend that same approach with your doctor, because otherwise it's way too easy to let him intimidate you into thinking he's always right. My dad, who never let anyone intimidate him into anything, had a great example of why this is necessary. He once refused a pill in the hospital because it looked unfamiliar. When the nurse grew testy at his recalcitrance, he demanded to see the doctor. His doc took one look at the pill and said, "You're right, that pill isn't for you!"

Now, I'm not trying to scare you, just to make a point. To get the health care that's best for *you,*

you've got to be pushy. Leave the etiquette to Miss Manners, ask a lot of questions and don't be afraid to say no. If you think you might have trouble being pushy:

- Take a friend along who can play the "bad cop" for you; or
- Say you'll get back to the doctor tomorrow on whether you want to have that procedure he's suggesting. That will buy you time to decide how *you* want to proceed.

THE ONLY DIFFERENCE BETWEEN A RUT AND A GRAVE IS THE DEPTH

4. *Take the home cure.* And then there's that "L" word: "lifestyle" (the health advocates' synonym for cigarettes, beer, red meat, dessert and couches). You knew it would come to this eventually, didn't you? Unfortunately, those bad old habits *under*mine you when it comes to your performance at work. The following story illuminates my point.

I saw a movie once that featured a really tall leading actress and a rather short leading man, and since such bi-level relationships weren't yet politically correct, the director went to great lengths to ameliorate the problem. He had the actress stand in a ditch whenever she and her love interest were side by side. Well, I knew that before I went, and (perhaps as a result) I thought I detected a chronic note of wistfulness, or remorse, in the actress's expression—as if perhaps her feet were wet, or she was worried that something might come crawling out of the ground.

That's what it's like going to work each day when you live an unhealthy lifestyle. Things that are beyond the range of your perception can take a toll on your performance—and you never know when something hidden under the surface will suddenly come up and bite. Not to mention the fact that it's a drag to go around with your feet in a ditch all day—especially one you've dug yourself.

So give a thought to changing those unhealthy habits.

- See if habit-control classes or other treatment options are offered (or paid for) by your employer: changing habits with professional support is often easier than doing it on your own.
- If you can't shake them for your own benefit, then change them for your family: after all, they're affected by your choices, too.

But I don't know why you should listen to me about any of this. I mean, if I'm such a health care expert, why was I playing cat and mouse in high school? And what was I expecting when I made that crack about my sister's collision? Well, live and learn. I was so much younger then. Thank heaven I'm older than that now.

The Working Wounded Poll

If you were the boss, what would be your approach to drug testing?

I'd say no to testing and stand tall, 17%
I'd only test if I had a darn good reason, that's
    my call, 35%
I'd say no to drugs and test them all, 48%

Poll conducted at *workingwounded.com*

from email to *workingwounded.com*

Bet You're Glad You Don't Work Where This Guy Does

My mission at work is to treat my co-workers and others well, and to leave this life with what I entered with—all the parts of my body.

from email to *workingwounded.com*

What Goes Down Must Come Up?

I'll tell you what gave me stress: getting a summer job as an elevator operator in a high-rise office building and then learning that I suffer EXPLO-SIVELY from motion sickness.

ACCORDING TO MY LAST STRESS TEST, I'M DEAD

Dear WW: *I bumped into a friend I hadn't seen in a while and he went on and on about how awful I looked. I know I've been under a lot of stress lately, but I didn't*

215

realize that it was so clear to everyone around me. Any tips on dealing with stress?

ALL SHOOK UP

Dear Shook,

Back in my old consulting days (before I got a real job) I met with one of the major airlines to help with a problem in their reservations center. The human resources director explained that the phone operators were required to take a certain number of phone calls each hour and at the same time meet specified sales quotas. "Gee, that sounds pretty stressful," I said. "How do you help them cope?" She rattled off a list of programs: "Lifestyle Management," "Ten Minutes to Perfection and Productivity," "Coffee, Tea or Prozac?" . . . I noticed that none of them mentioned stress. I expressed my surprise. "Oh," she said, "if employees knew that *we* knew how stressful their jobs are, they could probably sue us and win." "I see," I said slowly. "So your company's main strategy for dealing with stress is to eliminate the word?" The woman smiled at me apologetically. "Yes."

Well, don't we all wish it were so easy. Unfortunately stress doesn't disappear just by wishing it away. It takes a kind of personal reengineering effort to bring it under control. I've found the following strategies work for me. Maybe they'll work for you.

1. *Can you eliminate any of the factors that cause your stress?* I know what you're thinking: Of course not! That's why I'm stressed! But take a step back. Often with a broader perspective we find that some of the things we thought had to be done by us, right now, can actually be postponed . . . or delegated . . . or even (heaven forbid) not done. Stress expands geometrically with each new stressor. Fortunately, it shrinks geometrically, too.

2. *If you can't control your stressors, can you change your attitude about them?* To borrow the language of belly buttons: stress is caused as much by "innies" as by "outies." The way we *feel* about a stressor determines how stressful we think it is. I've found that I can control how stressed I feel about certain projects by reminding myself that, in the long term, they're taking me where I want to go. This doesn't relieve the stress—but it makes it easier to bear.

3. *Adopt the 80 percent standard.* You know the old maxim, anything worth doing is worth doing well? Well, sorry, mom, not always. Not all jobs require the same level of perfection. When you've got a million projects demanding your attention, prioritize. Do the less important ones at 80 percent, save 100 percent perfection for the biggies. Anything else is martyrdom.

And as any martyr knows, the alternative is a poor solution. Consider what Harpo said at Chico's funeral. When someone asked him how he felt, he shrugged and answered, "A lot better than Chico."

The Working Wounded Quotebook

Why don't we ever say "try softer."
LILY TOMLIN

The Working Wounded List

Uptight and Out of Sight . . . What Causes Stress at Work

1. I worry about my company's future, 55%
2. My job is secure if I perform well, 50%
3. I worry about being laid off, 46%
4. My workload is excessive, 44%
5. My job has too much pressure, 43%

from International Study Research Corporation
via *The Wall Street Journal*

from email to *workingwounded.com*

Baby, We Were Born to *Preach?*

I handle my stress on the way to work. Know any other ministers who arrive at church on a Harley-Davidson?

CAN I STAY HEALTHY UNDER MANAGED CARE?

Dear WW: *My employer just switched to an HMO. I don't like giving up my old doctor, and I'm afraid I won't get as good treatment.*

WHAT'S UP, DOC?

Dear What's,

A buddy of mine once bought a way-cool car. There was only one problem. He was always hitching rides in my old beater because between the breakdowns and the "hi-test" gas, his car was too rich for the road.

It was kind of like our health care system in the 1980s: a hotrod of a system that became too expensive to run. So here we are in the 1990s, leaping—

"I don't mean to grouse, but I had a
better HMO down there."

or being pushed—into some form of managed care. This means insurance companies have gone from being passive bill payers to calling the shots on many aspects of health care. From now on, you'll need to be more aggressive if you want to get the highest quality care.

For starters, read your contract (not to make my writing look snappy in comparison, but to help you understand the rules your new health provider is following). If you can decode the fine print (which the folks in personnel should be happy to help you with) you'll find out what limits the company has placed on your care, and perhaps even some ways to challenge their decisions. Next, swallow any intimidation those white coats give you and ask your doctor the following questions:

1. *Are there limits on what I can be told about treatment options?* These are commonly known as "gag orders" and they're much more serious than when your doctor takes the tongue depressor and makes you say "ahh." Under a gag order, medical staff are prohibited from telling you about treatments that aren't covered by your health plan. Most docs *aren't* covered by gag orders, but you want to know if yours is.

2. *Does your doc make money from any of the treatment he's recommending?* X rays, lab tests, prescriptions, even referrals to other doctors can earn *your* doc a kickback. You want to know if something other than your health is influencing his opinion. (Remember Dr. Mike's X rays?)

3. *Is your doctor compensated under a "capitated" plan?* Under "capitation" (couldn't they have picked a better word?) the insurance company pays your doc a set fee for you each month, regardless of what happens. Obviously, the less treatment you receive, the more money he gets. Proponents of capitation argue that providers don't undertreat their patients because limiting care creates more serious (read expensive) illness later on. But capitation's critics point out that insurance companies are more concerned about today's expenses

than tomorrow's (can you say "quarterly earnings"?), and therefore do have an incentive to restrict treatment. In any event, the doctors I talked to in preparing this column felt that too many doctors these days are cutting too many corners.

BMC (before managed care) you probably paid too much money for too many medical services. Now the challenge is making sure you get what you need. Most studies suggest that patients do— but that the burden falls on you to learn the rules, ask the tough questions and work the system. Don't let your new doctor substitute the hypocritic oath for the Hippocratic.

from email to *workingwounded.com*

I Went to Work and All I Got Was This Lousy T-shirt?

I'm the head of a substance abuse agency that recently contracted for health insurance through a managed care plan. Although the insurer didn't require it, I decided to take advantage of our insurance switch to require our employees to take ran-

dom drug tests. It was not a popular decision, so to help it go down better, I created a series of T-shirts. The first one said "Piss on Urinalysis." The second one showed a half-filled specimen bottle with the words "I Gave at the Office." It didn't make people happier about the situation—but it gave them something to wear on dress-down Fridays.

The Working Wounded Quiz

Under three of the situations described below your employer is required to continue to make health insurance available to you. Under which is your employer not required to make it available?
1. Your hours are reduced
2. You lose your job and your employer has only fifteen employees
3. You lose your job because you're inefficient
4. You lose your job due to negligence

Answer on page 333.

from email to *workingwounded.com*

The Secret to Being Happy, Healthy and More Productive

Spend as much time as possible in the bathroom. You get more peace and productivity there than anywhere else in the office.

HOW MUCH SHOULD YOU TRUST THE COMPANY DOCTOR?

Dear WW: *My company has an on-site health clinic for employees. I really like the doctor, but a friend told me I'm better off seeing an outside doctor (even though it means making a co-payment) than giving my health information to my company.*

SHOULD I TAKE MY PANTS OFF AT WORK?

Dear Pants,

From Marcus Welby to *ER*, we have a long tradition of physicians who cure whatever ails you (usually within the hour), who never send a bill and who always put you at the center of the drama. Unfortunately, corporate life isn't always like the little screen. If you work for a company that has an in-house medical clinic, the staff there may have a severe case of divided loyalties as they try to treat both you and the company's bottom line. Even routine check-ups can reveal information about you that you'd rather the company not know.

In "Can a Visit to the Company Doc Help a Cold but Hurt a Career?" by Deborah Jacobs (*New York Times,* May 21, 1995), a spokesman for Ford recommended that employees see a company doctor only for job-related injuries. All other conditions should be reserved for your personal physician. (Your personal doc is paid by the company's health plan, but it's unlikely that she would release your health records to your employer.) Privacy experts quoted in the article offered the following guidelines for deciding when to see the company doc and when to steer clear:

1. *Procedures that can be "safely" performed by the company physician:* These include job-related injuries, flu shots and most hearing tests. Little can come of these procedures that might cause your employer to consider you a liability.
2. *Procedures that could jeopardize your job:* These include blood pressure and cholesterol tests (unusually high scores could encourage your employer to dismiss you for fear of large medical bills down the road); cancer screenings (again, a positive response could generate concern about your long-term health care costs); and, amazing-

ly enough, allergy shots (your employer could overreact to your allergy and restrict the type of work you do).

3. *Procedures that should never be done by a company physician:* These include genetic screening and HIV tests (no surprise here), but also urinalysis. According to the privacy pros, sharing urinalysis results with your boss is like "throwing your medical chart on someone's desk."

And what's so bad about that? It's generally illegal for employers to discriminate against employees based on information from their medical records—but (gasp!) it happens: employees have been fired for having expensive diseases (they've just been told they were sacked for something else). And while, sure, you could sue if you were fired (just when you really needed the paycheck and the insurance), the chance that you'd want to (or could afford to) is pretty slim.

So what it all boils down to is this: don't risk big-time trouble to avoid a small co-payment. Go to the doc when you need to—just not one who's a fellow employee. Now that CFOs' knives are as sharp as surgeons', an ounce of privacy may be worth a pound of continued employment.

The Working Wounded List

Dying to Get the Job Done . . . Jobs with the Highest Rate of Death

1. Fisherman
2. Logger
3. Pilot
4. Miner
5. Structural metal worker

from U.S. Bureau of Labor Statistics, 1995

from email to *workingwounded.com*

Per Orders of the Company Doc: Please Remain Seated for the Safety Lecture

A company trying to continue its five-year perfect safety record showed its workers a film aimed at encouraging the use of safety goggles on the job. According to Industrial Machinery News, *the film's depiction of gory industrial accidents was so graphic that twenty-five workers suffered minor injuries in their rush to leave the screening room. Thirteen others fainted, and one man required seven stitches after he cut his head falling off a chair while watching the film.*

from *News of the Weird* by Chuck Shepherd et al. (Plume, 1989)

The Working Wounded Quotebook

66 99

The time to relax is when you don't have the time.

SIDNEY LEWIS

HOW TO SPOT AND TREAT CARPAL TUNNEL SYNDROME

Dear WW: *Last night I woke up at 3:00 A.M with a sharp pain in my forearm. My husband says I'm dreaming, but I think that it's from typing all day at work. Is there an easy way for me to tell if all that typing is doing me in?*

I'M TYPING AS FAST AS I CAN

"And, as a new employee, you are immediately entitled
to participate in the company's proactive health plan."

Dear Typing,

I saw a cartoon once that had a guy looking into a long tunnel. His face was frozen in a look that somehow combined hope, bewilderment and fear. The caption read, "Upon realizing that the light at the end of the tunnel was a train."

Now I don't want to be an alarmist, but you may be looking down a similar tunnel of your own—the *carpal* tunnel—because you've got one of the early signs of carpal tunnel syndrome: burning pain during noncomputer time. Other warning signs are dull achiness, tenderness when touched, radiating pain, numbness and tingling, loss of muscle coordination, and stiffness. Now for the good news: serious damage can be prevented, but you'll have to act fast. Visit an ergonomist, physical therapist or doctor and have it checked out. (And if you can pronounce "ergonomist," that and a buck should get you a cup of coffee.)

Here's a short explanation of repetitive strain injuries, courtesy of Ian Chong, a Seattle-based ergonomist. The wrist is a pretty busy place: you've got tendons, bones and a nerve all squeezed into a small area known as the carpal tunnel. If the tendons are forced to stretch at funny angles all day, as they often are when you type, they can get inflamed and swell up, putting pressure on the nerve. (And nerves like pressure even less than your customers do.)

Another kind of pressure will begin to mount on corporations if the $5.3 million decision against Digital Equipment Corporation is upheld. (They were sued for making keyboards that allegedly caused carpal tunnel syndrome.) But more important than winning a lawsuit is preventing injuries before they start. I've adapted the following tips from *Zap!* by Don Sellers (Peachpit Press, 1994).

1. *Can you avoid long stretches of repetitive movement?*
   My wife, who writes all day, keeps worry beads and a ball by the side of her computer. No, she's

not a Cubs fan: they're tools she uses to exercise her hands. She also breaks up typing with phone calls, errands and stretches so her arms get a break.

2. *Can you minimize the bending of your wrists as you type?* Tendons are happiest when your wrists are level and your fingers are pointed straight at the keyboard, perpendicular to your torso.

3. *Can you stretch your arms and fingers during the workday?* Every interruption, lunch break, bathroom break and phone call is an opportunity to flex your wrists, wiggle your fingers, shake out your arms and otherwise relax and loosen that wrist area.

Your job may not send you down the tunnel of love, but, hopefully, if you follow the advice above, it won't send you down the carpal tunnel either.

The Working Wounded Quotebook

The graveyard is full of indispensable men.
CHARLES DE GAULLE

from email to *workingwounded.com*

Sometimes You've Got to Fish *and* Cut Bait . . .

You don't know what it's like to be "sick" about your job 'till you've worked the "slime line" in a fresh frozen fish packing plant for close to minimum wage. During the peak of the salmon season we would work from 8:00 A.M. until midnight, wearing oversized rain gear, standing along a conveyer belt that was flooded with cold running water, scraping guts out of fish with a metal spoon. By the end of the shift it would look like a horror movie set, and on heavy production days we would be ankle deep in fish innards. After all this, they served us fish on Fridays.

RESPONDING TO A COLLEAGUE WHO HAS AIDS

Dear WW: *A man who I work closely with and like a lot just confided to me that he has AIDS. I'm shocked and I don't know how to respond.*

SCARED

232

Dear Scared,

You can catch a lot of things at work—a cold, things falling through the cracks or hell. But AIDS is one of the few things you *can't* catch—unless you and your co-worker work the way Demi Moore and Michael Douglas did in *Disclosure*. So start by letting go of the fear that you might somehow get it from him.

The next step is to start thinking about how you can support your co-worker. Try asking yourself a few questions.

1. *Suppose he'd told you he had cancer: how would you respond?* AIDS is a disease, not a judgment. Spend less time thinking about how he got infected and more time being compassionate.

2. *For just a moment, can you see through the eyes of your colleague?* Understandably you feel afraid. But if you really want to know fear, imagine that you have an immune deficiency disease, that you're continuing to work, in part, to keep your health benefits, and that the person at the next desk comes to work with a cold. That person's inconvenience and runny nose is, to you, a possible medical emergency.

3. *Can you listen to your co-worker?* That may be what he needs above all: to feel that you can respond to him just as you did before: nonjudgmentally—as a friend, as a colleague, as a person.

4. *Are you operating with an outdated image of AIDS?* These days, new drug therapies are extending people's lives and keeping their symptoms sufficiently minimized that many can remain in the workplace indefinitely. So continue to think of this person as a productive colleague, not as a person with a terminal disease.

As you look toward the future of working with this man there are three additional things you can do—in fact, *have* to do—because people with AIDS are legally protected under the Americans with Disabilities Act (ADA).

1. *Maintain his confidence.* If he asked you to keep his diagnosis secret, you must do so. His confidentiality is protected by the ADA.
2. *Offer him a helping hand.* Offering help to coworkers with AIDS is legally mandated by the ADA. Are there things you can do to help your colleague remain productive?
3. *Stand up for him.* Many people still aren't open-minded or educated about AIDS. Fearing discrimination (including loss of employment and benefits), your colleague is probably not in a position to lobby or educate others. Those of us who can must rally in their stead. Contact your local AIDS organization or public health department for suggestions.

Researchers have made tremendous strides against AIDS in the past few years, and the future promises more. Now let's make the same kind of inroads against its companion disease: bias against the people who have it.

The Working Wounded Toolbox

What We Can All Learn from AIDS . . . Common Traits of AIDS Survivors

- Grit, pluck and the courage to face up to almost anything
- Spirituality combined with irreverence
- The feeling of being chosen for an important mission

from *Parade Magazine* (January 31, 1993)

CHAPTER 9

STUCK IN THE WEB

*How to Score Points
with Technology*

I MET MY MATCH

Has the glut of new technology got you feeling like you're always a couple of points behind and scrambling to even the score? Well, a while ago I found a way to stay on top of the high-tech game. Surprisingly, I learned it while I was still a senior in high school . . .

Back then I was considered the best boys tennis player in the school. Unfortunately, this was more a comment on the caliber of tennis in Boonton, New Jersey, than an endorsement of my ability on the court. But it was an achievement, nonetheless, and I felt it only fitting that I defend my manhood and challenge the best girls player, Maureen, to a match. I was pretty confident about winning: I had a killer serve, a solid net game and a wicked slice. There was no way Maureen could win. I told her so as soon as she accepted my challenge—but she just smiled at me demurely and murmured, "We'll see."

The day of the match I got to the court early and was practicing overhead smashes when Maureen arrived. She sat on the bench and watched as I blasted one ball after another over the net. When I felt that I'd intimidated her adequately I stopped, made a big production of wiping the sweat from my forehead, and walked over to the bench. As I approached she stood up and handed me a single rose.

"What's that for?" I asked.

"I just wanted to give you this so you'd take it easy on me. Remember, it's not nice to beat up on a girl."

You could have heard the testosterone draining from my toes. With a single rose Maureen had me where she wanted me: in an excruciating double bind. If I played hard and won I'd be a bully. If I lost, I'd be a wimp. It was a no-win situation.

But apparently Maureen wasn't done playing with my head. As I watched, she unzipped her racquet bag and pulled out a brand-new Prince racquet—one of those oversized jobs that had just come onto the market and that my tennis buddies and I had made fun of in the store. Only losers would use those racquets, we'd guffawed, people who needed an extra mile or two of racquet head in order to hit the ball. Well, suddenly the Prince didn't look so foolish; it looked like a gaping maw primed to find and return every one of my balls.

Maureen smiled at me sweetly. "With your serve I figured I'd need some extra help," she said, and the very sweetness of her voice told me she didn't believe a word of it. At that moment, the competition ended. The match itself was a mere formality. As I recall she beat me 6–3, 6–1.

So what does "Bob's last stand" on the tennis court have to do with technology at work? Plenty— because my little encounter with Maureen is the perfect illustration of T&A. (No, not that kind of T&A!) I'm talking about Tools and Attitude. Maureen beat me not because she was a better player (though she might tell a different story), but because her Tools and her Attitude put her on top. And that's what the right T&A can do for you. They can help you use technology to stay competitive in today's complex work environment.

THIS KIND OF T&A CAN HELP YOU AT WORK

How? Let's start with the Tools. I don't have to tell you that there are lots of them out there: computers, cell phones, email, the Internet, video, personal digital assistants . . . not to mention all the software that goes with them. Unfortunately, I can't tell you which tools and software will make you more productive, happier, healthier and better-looking. (But if *you* find one that makes you better-looking please email me immediately!) The answer to that depends on you, your job, your competitors, your problems, your budget and numerous other individual factors. What I can tell you, though, is that you have to be open to *all* the technological possibilities. Because like it or not, they're changing the way we work. If you want to stay on top, you have to think creatively about your business—about how high tech can improve your effectiveness and efficiency—then you have to invest time in learning about all of the latest gadgets. Because whether *you* do or not, your competitors *will* (and I mean competitors for your business *or* that promotion you've been coveting)—and that can put you at a serious disadvantage.

I learned that from Maureen. Oh, I fought it all right. For years I refused to believe that that oversized, "cheater's" racquet would change the way tennis was played. But even traditionalists change . . . Fortunately I've come around quicker on the technology front—though I know plenty of people who haven't. I know a manager at the local phone company, for instance, who swore he'd never let his employees start telecommuting because he'd have no idea what they were doing. Well, three months later his company made telecommuting an option and now the guy's forced to . . . well . . . "reevaluate" his position. I also know a bookstore that refused to sell products over the Internet because they doubted the security of online transactions. Now *Amazon.com* ("the world's largest bookstore") has captured a larger share of the market and they're scrambling to develop an online presence. The reality is, change happens, even to the reluctant. That's why you've got to keep your Attitude open and your Tools up to date.

FOLLOW THESE POINTERS AND YOU'LL BE JUMPING OVER THE NET

It's helpful, actually, to approach technology as if it were a game of tennis. And the following tips are guaranteed to help you score:

1. *Start at "love."* (Or at least at "like.") That's how a tennis game starts: love is the zero score. And since technology is here to stay, you might as well make love your starting point, too. Sound like a tough assignment? Then think of high-tech tools as toys. Browse in a computer store

once in a while just to play the games. Surf the Web once a month just to see what's there. Visit a video arcade occasionally to see how wild computer graphics have become. Technology's your chance to be a kid again. Grab it.

2. *Do warm-ups.* For my first year as a columnist I used my computer like a glorified typewriter while I meticulously counted the words in my column by hand. Dumb, huh? But I'd never taken the time to find out what my computer could do. Spare yourself that problem by doing warm-ups. Take the time to practice with your machines—to flex their muscles, if you will—so that you know *all* the ways they can help you work.

3. *Cover your court.* You can't win at tennis if you're standing in one place, and the same is true in business. You need to investigate every corner of your enterprise to learn how technology can improve it. Is data always slow, for instance, when it travels between two departments? Is inventory tracked as effectively as possible? Would certain workers' productivity increase if they telecommuted from another location? Cover every area so you can respond to the latest need.

4. *Keep your eye on the ball.* Pretty basic, huh? No matter *how* big your racquet head is, you can't hit the ball if you haven't seen it coming. Well, ditto with technology. You can't use technology

to meet your needs if you're not aware of what's out there. That means you need to make a point of reading the technology columns in the business press (*Fortune, Inc., Fast Company, Business Week*), in your industry magazines and in your local paper. They should help you to stay current.

5. *Change your game as necessary.* There's nothing like complacency to kill a winning streak. You know how it works: you figure out your opponent's game and settle into a routine, then *wham!* she changes it and you're left scrambling. Well, don't let that happen with technology. Once you've invested in new technology, don't assume it will work forever. Needs and technology change, so keep looking for the next best thing. Don't find yourself playing last year's game.

6. *Run for every ball (even the ones that seem too far away).* Sure, you'll land on your elbow sometimes, but you'll return a lot more balls. My wife used to tease me for always buying the latest toy. In some ways she was right: the first Apple "portable" was more aptly nicknamed the "luggable." That Newton paperweight on my desk was probably also a waste of money. But my fascination with the Internet ultimately landed me a job as a Web consultant despite my lack of background in the high-tech field. So don't be afraid to take a flier on technology that seems

remote. The more you pursue, the greater your chance of return.

If you do all these things you'll be scoring like the pros. As for myself, you wouldn't believe how my game has improved since I started playing with a larger racquet. Maureen, if you're reading this, I'm ready for a rematch. Email me.

The Working Wounded Poll

If someone wants to get your attention, what's the best way to do it?

Fax, 13%
Voice mail, 27%
Email, 58%

Poll conducted at *workingwounded. com*

from email to *workingwounded. com*

I Don't Remember Seeing *This* in Any Computer Ads

My computer has doubled my productivity. Now I can play twice as much computer solitaire at work.

The Working Wounded List

How Do You Know That
You Bought a Bad Computer?

- Lower corner of the screen has the words "Etch-A-Sketch" on it
- Only chip inside is a Dorito
- You catch a virus from it

from *David Letterman's Book of Top Ten Lists* (Bantam, 1996)

IS THE INTERNET A REAL BUSINESS TOOL OR A TOY?

Dear WW: *I'm the marketing VP for a manufacturing company. My CEO came in this week and told me he wanted a Web site right away. His kid's fourth-grade class has its own homepage and his kid is teasing him because his company doesn't. I don't even own a modem . . .*

STUCK IN MY OWN WEB

Dear Stuck,

I remember the day in grammar school when my pal Mark asked, "If a tree fell in the forest and

244

"Be patient, madam. At this very moment, high-speed computers are working to eliminate or aggravate your problem."

no one heard it, would it make a noise?" We'd never heard that one before and it promptly divided the class into camps: those who felt it would make a noise; those who felt it wouldn't; those who couldn't figure out why a perfectly good tree would suddenly fall; and those who were too busy shooting spitballs to care. Well, the Internet is like that forest—and the question for you is: will your Net efforts be heard?

The answer is probably yes, because despite its miserable faddishness, the Internet's here to stay and it's changing the way we do business. So get a modem and start surfing. I'd also check out *The*

Internet Strategy Handbook (edited by Mary Cronin, HBS Press, 1996), which reveals the Internet strategy of major corporations including Dow Jones, Digital Equipment and others. The following questions can help to focus your efforts:

1. *Why do you need a presence on the Internet?* Companies mainly use the Net to sell products and to disseminate information (product brochures, price lists, service info and so on). But that's not the real beauty of the Web. Its greatest benefit is its interactivity. Your customers can talk back! That means they can tell you what they're interested in, what they like and don't like about your products, services and prices, and how you can serve them better. It's an ear to the ground that you can update at a moment's notice at minimal cost.

2. *Who are you trying to reach?* The Internet is your ultimate opportunity to narrowcast. Once Web visitors tell you their interests, your site can automatically route them to the information they'll be most interested in. Which means that if you take the time to analyze your audience, you can deliver remarkably targeted pitches to each of your sub-markets quickly and efficiently.

3. *Can you make money from the Web?* Most Web sites are money-losers (or loss leaders, as their Webmasters like to say). But, increasingly, com-

panies *will* make money—by selling products, by selling information acquired from visitors to their sites and by selling ads. Can you sell your products on the Web? Are there companies that might want to advertise on your site in order to reach your customers? Neither avenue is likely to produce income right away, but if you start developing them now, you'll be well positioned in the future when the market heats up.

These days it seems that the Internet is the answer no matter what the question. But if you look past the hype I think you'll find a cost-effective way to interact with the key constituencies of your business. So start surfing, and as you're hanging ten (fingers, that is) keep track of the sites you like and note who developed them. If you decide to make the leap to the Net you'll already have a list of people whose work you admire. But if you still need more help, there's a certain fourth-grade class . . .

from email to *workingwounded.com*

I Think It's Already Taken

My company should adopt the following as its motto: "Using yesterday's technology to solve today's problems—tomorrow."

from email to *workingwounded.com*

They Went That-a-Way!

Why is it that whenever you call a software company the problem is always with the hardware, and when you call a hardware company the problem is always with the software?

The Working Wounded Toolbox

Stuck on the Information Superhighway? . . . The Biggest Problems of the Net

1. Slow access, 73%
2. Information difficult to locate, 66%
3. Difficult connections, 61%
4. High cost, 56%
5. Content isn't interesting, 36%

Louis Harris poll via "Internet Troubles Aren't Fed Up—Yet" by Keith Hammonds (*Business Week*, August 26, 1996)

WHAT ARE THE SECRETS TO SUCCESS ON THE NET?

Dear WW: *We've had a Web site up for a few months and I feel like we've fallen into a black hole. The site hasn't generated any business for us. I know it's dumb to pull the plug, but I'm beginning to lose my patience.*
STUCK IN A POTHOLE ON THE INFO HIGHWAY

Dear Stuck:

To paraphrase Woody Allen, when it comes to the Internet, 80 percent of life is *not* just showing up. Success requires showing up *and* filling a need. Which reminds me of my wife and her cousin, who couldn't be further apart when it comes to their views of the Internet. Amy just loves it. She's been to the Louvre, gets her weather directly from the satellite and was the first on her block to see Madonna's baby pictures. My wife, on the other hand, believes the real reason they call it the Net is because that's what you feel trapped in every time you visit. So one day they made a bet about who could find the Blue Book value of my wife's 1986 Volvo first. My wife called a local used-car lot and got the number in seven minutes. After two hours on the Information Superhighway her cousin had yet to flag down anything.

For all the hype, the Internet these days is still a chaotic, crowded, bumpy road. But there's a lot you can do to make it a smoother ride for you and the people who visit your stretch of it. The following questions have been adapted from *The Digital Estate* by Charles Martin (McGraw-Hill, 1997).

1. *Can people find your site?* Or are you one of those companies that spends huge amounts on the Web and then doesn't advertise their URL (an address on the Internet—otherwise known as the hieroglyphics following the ubiquitous http://) on all their marketing material, stationery and business cards?

2. *Once there, can people get what they need in a minute or less?* Although most surfers are now on unlimited-access plans, you've still got to treat their time as precious (remember there are lots of other sites to visit besides yours). Follow the "three-click rule": visitors should be able to get the information they need in three clicks or less.

3. *Does everything at your site have a price tag?* It's tough to make a fast buck on the Net. Heck, it's even tough to make a slow buck! So instead, *give away* everything you can. Making your site less of a salesroom and more of a resource room can bring you real business down the road.

4. *Are there opportunities for audience participation?* The Internet is a twenty-four-hour a day, seven-day-a-week focus group. Use surveys, contests

and chats to learn about your audience and how to better serve it.

5. *Does it offer something to people who don't have the latest technology?* Before you get too addicted to fancy graphics that take forever to download remember that there are lots of people out there with 14.4 modems. Always view your site from a variety of modem speeds.

There is one small detail that I left out about the bet between my wife and her cousin. Although my wife got the value of the car in only seven minutes it took her another forty-two to get the used-car salesman off the phone. On second thought, maybe the Net isn't so bad after all.

from email to *workingwounded.com*

This Gives a Whole New Meaning to "Hair Net"

As part of a job interview, I was asked to demonstrate that I knew how to navigate and download something off the Internet. So with shaking hands and more than a prayer or two, I went online, accessed some data and then tried to print it out. Immediately the printer jammed. I leaned over to straighten the paper and voilà, it came unstuck. The good news: it finally printed what I'd asked it to. The bad news: it was printing on my hair. I screamed and the boss ran over to shut it off. Believe it or not they still gave me the job.

The Working Wounded Quotebook **""**

Computers are useless. They can only give you the answers.

PICASSO

The Working Wounded Quiz

Can your employer monitor your personal phone calls at work?

Answer on page 333.

CAN YOUR BOSS READ YOUR EMAIL?

Dear WW: *I know this will sound paranoid, but last week my boss said something to me that he could only have known if he had been reading my email. Isn't the* *privacy of my email at work protected just like my phone calls are?*

BUGGED

Dear Bugged,

There is an old rule of journalism that Working Wounded always follows: when paraphrasing someone famous, make sure the person is dead. Better yet: make sure their lawyers are dead, too. So, with apologies to Shakespeare (who has been dead for several centuries—which still isn't enough for the average high school student), I offer you this ditty:

Friends, Romans, co-workers, lend me your ears.
I come to bury privacy, not to praise it.
The email that workers do lives after them;
It is not protected like their phones.

The truth about email privacy is that there isn't any. Big Brother is here—in the form of your employer—and he is legally permitted complete access to your email. The courts so far have ruled that since the corporation owns the equipment over which the email is sent, they also own access to all its content. According to the *New York Times* ("Who's Reading Your Email? Maybe the Boss" by Patrice Duggan Samuels, May 12, 1996), the Society for Human Resource Management (an HR trade organization) suggests companies ask employees to sign a form which says, "I am aware that the company reserves, and will exercise, the right to review, audit, intercept, access and disclose all matters on the company's Email system at any time, with or without employee notice, and that such access may occur during or after working hours."

For those of you who think hitting the delete key will solve the problem—think again. Although the file may disappear from your computer screen, it doesn't disappear entirely. It just moves to a delete folder where it can be accessed any time by your company.

So unless you want your email messages strung up around the office like so much dirty laundry, ask yourself the following questions before you hit "send."

1. *Does my company have an email policy?* Policies, when they exist, vary widely. Intel's policy permits routine email monitoring; Apple's policy places employee email off limits. Grab your dusty old personnel manual and see if your company has a policy. If there's nothing on email, play it safe and assume that your company's philosophy is closer to Intel's than Apple's.

2. *Do nonemployees have access to your company's email?* According to Judd Lees, an attorney with Williams, Kastner and Gibbs (Bellevue, Washington), employers may be prohibited from reviewing employees' email without the employees' consent *if* the system is also accessed

by nonemployees (he bases his interpretation on the Electronic Communications Privacy Act of 1986).

3. *Would you be comfortable having your email appear in the company newsletter?* There's probably only one thing in life that's immortal—a dumb missive you wrote to a co-worker in a fit of anger, or even worse, bratty comments about your boss. So unless you want these puppies nipping at your heels for the rest of your career, don't send it via email.

Who knows? Maybe the policies will change. Employee phone privacy is protected; perhaps in the future we'll get the same protection for our written words. But for the moment, I again refer you to the Bard, who (with no paraphrasical help from me) called the tune four hundred years ago: "The better part of valor is discretion . . ."

The Working Wounded List

It's Like Leaving Your Keys in the Car—Most Commonly Used Computer Passwords

1. Your first, last or kid's name
2. "Secret"

3. Stress–related words ("deadline," "work")
4. Sports teams or terms ("Bulls," "golfer")
5. "Payday"
6. "Bonkers"
7. The current season ("winter," "spring")
8. Your ethnic group
9. Repeated characters ("aaaaa," "bbbbb")
10. Obscenities, sexual terms

Deloitte & Touche via "Hackers Delight"
(*Business Week*, February 10, 1997)

The Working Wounded List

Please Don't Copy Any of These Tricks . . . How Employees Abuse Copy Machines

- Using copier's glass surface to heat pastries
- Letting pet gerbils escape from their cage and build a nest in copier
- Trying to copy coins by putting them through automatic feeder
- A frustrated sheriff's deputy taking out his gun and shooting it

from U.S. Office Equipment contest via "Out of Order"
(*Fortune*, March 3, 1997)

"I got your email. I'm going to email you now."

ARE YOU STUCK IN AN ELECTRONIC TRAFFIC JAM?

Dear WW: *Last week I received over three hundred email messages! I complained to my boss, who promptly told me to come up with recommendations to reduce the number of emails sent within our company. I don't have a clue as to what we can do about it.*

STUCK IN AN ELECTRONIC TRAFFIC JAM

Dear Stuck,

Your letter reminded me of an old friend's Vietnam War story. When his base became the target of a mortar attack, there were, thankfully, few casualties. But one thing that took a direct hit was the compressor of the officers' club refrigerator. Well, the enlisted men thought their prayers had been answered: at dinner that night their plates were loaded with lobster. The next morning lobster was nestling amidst their powdered eggs. The situation began to seem less sublime, however, when lobster showed up again at lunch . . . and then again at dinner . . . and then regularly on the menu for the better part of a week. My friend tells me he has since come to terms with his tour in Vietnam, but *not* with lobster.

So what's the connection between lobster and email? In the right amounts, they're both a delicacy. Trouble is, some people believe that if a little is good, then a lot must be better. So they serve it up in mammoth portions. Minutes from committees we didn't know existed, messages from people we've never even heard of . . . Finally we get so bloated from the overload we can only sit around and groan.

Well, congratulations. Your boss has handed you the mandate to create Overemailers Anonymous. You can now put your company on an email diet. To do so, ask your colleagues to consider the following questions. I've adapted them from *Business Wisdom of the Electronic Elite* by Geoffrey James (Times Books, 1996).

1. *Who needs it?* Before email, it actually took time and effort to communicate. Imagine how much email volume would drop if FYI'ing took more than the touch of a "send" key? Before you press that button ask yourself honestly: "Does the recipient really need to see this?"

2. *Can you condense it?* You know why journalists put the most important stuff up front? Because most people never make it to the end. Keep that in mind next time you write an email. Get to the point ASAP, and make your message ASAP (as *short* as possible). This is especially important now that many people have software that lets them scan the first two lines of emails without opening the entire message.

3. *Can you give it a better name?* Emails give you room for a "subject" or "headline," and there's a reason. A well-chosen headline prepares the recipient for what she's about to read. It tells the reader if the message really needs her time. *And* it gets your message a greater chance of getting read.

4. *Can you do an archaeological dig in your in-box?* Sort through your email to determine how much of it is unnecessary, then share your results

with your colleagues. This should provide powerful ammunition to your argument that everyone needs to make his emailing more strategic.

Hopefully, after they've read your recommendations, your colleagues will be less generous when they dish out email. But tell them if they do, they can always send a question or comment to Working Wounded. We never tire of email—or lobster for that matter.

from email to *workingwounded.com*

So Much for the Paperless Office

Forgive me, father, for I have sinned . . . I take a copy of all my email and, by subject, I put it in a three-ring binder for later reading. Why read off a computer screen when there's still good old-fashioned paper you can use?

The Working Wounded Quotebook

Men have become the tools of their tools.
THOREAU

from email to *workingwounded.com*

The *Real* Revenge of the Nerds

I can't believe that those dorky AV guys in high school—the ones with the plastic pen cases and tape on their glasses—are now all worth millions. Who knew that if I'd only acquired an interest in overhead projectors back then, I'd be a millionaire today?

HOW DO YOU MANAGE SOMEONE YOU CAN'T SEE?

Dear WW: *My boss wanted to score points with his boss so he volunteered my department to be our company's telecommuting pilot program. I've tried to talk him out of it but it's no use.*

PHONE FROM HOME? *NO WAY!*

Dear Phone,

I was dense when it came to fifth-grade science. "Is there a hole in the middle of the wire that the electricity goes through?" I asked, "or do the little electrons crawl along the outside of the wire?" I can still see the frustration etched on Mr. Lee's face, fully aware that I was full of even dumber questions.

Just as I struggled with how electricity travels over electric wires, many bosses wonder how their management skills will travel over phone lines. "Out of sight . . . *are you out of your mind?*" is the reaction of most of the managers I've interviewed. To them, telecommuting is like America Online's first attempt to create an unlimited Internet access plan—great in theory but worse than useless if you wanted a productive connection.

For all of them—and you—I recommend *Making Telecommuting Happen* (Van Nostrand Reinhold, 1994) by Jack Nilles, the man who's been called the "father of telecommuting." It includes an entire section on how to manage someone you can't see. The following questions have been adapted from it:

1. *Have you carefully identified the people and projects for your pilot program?* Just like spandex, telecommuting isn't for everybody. Look for people who are disciplined, motivated, independent and who want to try working at home. Also, look for projects that can be completed in relative isolation.

2. *How will you know if they're working?* You won't, unless you establish specific and measurable out-

comes for each telecommuter and check in regularly. The irony, of course, is that some of the people currently under your "watchful eye" are probably spending time socializing, playing solitaire or surfing the Net. It just *looks* like they're working. Come to think of it, you might want to develop specific and measurable job outcomes for *all* your employees. What a concept!

3. *Can you manage someone you can't see?* Effective management involves communication and rapport—and, chances are, both will be harder to maintain when face-to-face contact is minimized. Nilles suggests you send routine information electronically and save complex or emotional information for face-to-face meetings.

4. *Can you keep them informed about what is going on back at the office?* Successful telecommuting programs suggest workers be brought into the office regularly for meetings and social events. *Social events?* Yes. People need formal *and* informal networks to do their job and feel part of the team. Believe it or not, it's good business to occasionally let them eat cake.

I stood on a downtown street corner and surveyed office workers about what they liked most about telecommuting. The top vote-getter: "the ability to work in your underwear." So in the finest journalistic tradition I wrote this entire column in my boxers. I can conclusively report that working in your underwear *is* cool. Of course, I might feel differently in winter.

from email to *workingwounded.com*

He Managed to Turn High Tech into No Tech

I do desktop publishing for a health care company. Every afternoon, the sun puts a glare on my computer screen and makes it virtually impossible to see, so I taped a piece of cardboard to the monitor. That worked nicely, but a few days later my boss told me to take it down. Why? Because the CEO has a policy that says you can't put anything on your computer. So I put in a purchase order for a $17 glare guard. After several months I still hadn't heard anything about it so I went up to the purchasing department. It turns out my $17 purchase request had gone all the way to the company's CFO—the guy who manages our company's billion-dollar budget—and he had denied it. Apparently our company is more concerned about how a computer looks than about what you can accomplish with it.

The Working Wounded Toolbox

The Following Is Guaranteed to Make You Feel Smarter About Today's Technology

Compaq is considering changing the command "Press Any Key" to "Press Return Key" because of the flood of calls asking where the "Any" key is.

The Working Wounded Quotebook

We are drowning in information but starved for knowledge.

JOHN NAISBITT

SHOVED OUT THE DOOR

*How to Survive a Layoff
or Firing*

YOU CAN GET THERE FROM HERE

It may *seem* like the end of the road, but there *is* life—and a career—after you've been fired or laid off. Sometimes you just need to go down a bit before you can go back up. And that reminds me of an experience I once had in Chicago . . .

I'd worked for ten years as a human resources consultant to corporations, and while the million frequent flier miles were good, my life was on hyperdrive. With clients splayed all over the map, I felt like a glob of mercury in a high school science experiment: diffused into a thousand drops. So you can imagine my joy when I acquired two clients in the very same building, the Sears Tower in

Chicago. No bumpy airline flight; no mad dash in a cab. This day, I'd be only thirty-seven floors from my next destination.

"Can you tell me how to get to the seventy-second floor?" I asked the receptionist after I'd finished with client number one.

She gave me a patronizing smile. "You can't get there from here."

"I beg your pardon?"

"I said you can't get there from here."

For a fraction of a second I believed her. Then I realized what she meant. "You mean these elevators don't go there?"

"That's right. You have to go down to the lobby and take the next bank of elevators to the sixtieth floor, then switch to the elevators that go to the seventy-second floor."

I pushed the button for the elevator and as the doors closed behind me I breathed a sigh of relief. The world of fundamental logic hadn't suddenly changed: I *could* get there from here. I'd just need a little detour to pull it off.

Well, not long after that my friend David got fired. As we talked about what had happened and mulled his prospects for the future, the receptionist's words came to mind—because I realized that that was how David felt. He could imagine a rosier future—a future with a satisfying job. But sitting in my living room in tremendous pain, he felt as if he couldn't get there from here.

NO NEED TO PRESS THE ALARM BUTTON

I understood that feeling: I'd felt it, too, once, after I'd been let go. And other friends had described a similar set of feelings. We simply had too much emotion—too much anger, too much distrust and way too much self-doubt—to believe that we were as valuable to an employer as we were before the dirty deed. We couldn't believe that our skills were the same, that our integrity was unchanged, or that the event that had led to our termination wouldn't poison our future employment.

But what we eventually discovered was that termination doesn't mean a horrible downward slide. As happened in Chicago, some of us had to go down a few floors before working our way back up. But our ascents were faster the second time around because of our accumulated experience, and ultimately we each reached—or surpassed—our original destinations.

So if you've been fired or laid off and you feel like the floor's giving way beneath your feet—don't hit the panic button. And don't despair of reaching the top. Because, despite what the pessimists say, you *can* get there from here. Here are some tips for making it happen.

HOW TO RISE AGAIN

1. *Stop at the Human Resources floor.* The first thing to do is negotiate a severance package—the best and biggest one you can get. You've bled and sweated for your company; now it's time to get paid back!

   I didn't get a severance package when I was fired. (I was too dumb to ask.) But a senior executive I know got one, and it was a beaut. Stan had worked for his company for twenty-seven years, and was as hardworking and loyal as they come. He figured his future was assured. What he didn't count on was getting a new boss. But as fate (and company politics) would have it, his old boss left and the new one's first priority was cleaning house. Stan was number one to go. His severance: six months pay with no benefits. Stan was devastated; he was also scared. He was over fifty, he had highly specialized skills and he had never really looked for a job. What was he going to do? Over lunch the next day Stan bemoaned his situation to a friend, and this executive, outraged at Stan's dismissal, spoke to the head of

personnel. Two days later the company presented Stan an amended severance package: full
salary and benefits for a year, counseling to help
him find another job and use of an office for the
length of his transition. Hard to believe? Yes,
considering how little it took to get the company to change its mind. No, when you consider
the guilt the company felt at dismissing a loyal,
senior employee. Guilt? You read it right—just
because they laid him off didn't mean that they
weren't interested in doing what they could to
get him back on his feet.

Now, you may not have Stan's seniority—or
his level of friends—but you can learn from his
story, nonetheless. You can learn that you don't
know what your company will give until you
ask. So ask! Here are some things you can ask
for. Get more ideas by talking to others in your
company who were terminated, or to an attorney. (Most will give you a half-hour consulta-
tion, plus sales pitch, for free.)

- *A letter of recommendation, a promise of good referrals and input on the timing and conditions of your
  exit.* These things are free to your employer,
  but invaluable to you.
- *Temporary health and life insurance, outplacement
  assistance and some reimbursement for job-hunting
  costs.* These things are cheaper for your
  employer than they are for you.

- *Cash.* A week's salary for each year of employment is fairly typical—but, Stan eventually got more and so might you. Again, you won't know till you ask.

2. *Press the UP button.* Once you've negotiated your severance, let go and move on. And I mean move on. Let go of the anger, the resentment and the feeling that it wasn't fair, and move ahead. Because the longer you look backward the longer it will take to get where you want to go.

   Put an end to that free-fall feeling by pushing the button that says UP. Focus on where you were going before the termination happened and plan how to get back on track. Which companies are the next logical stop in your career? Who do you know who can help you plot a way inside? Chapter 6 ("Struggling to Get Out") is full of tips for landing a new job. Read it and plan your next stop.

3. *Prepare your rap before you make your first stop.* Once you know where you want to work next, you'll have to make a decision: how (or whether) to tell your prospective employer that you were fired or laid off. Now, it may not feel like a choice. I know when I was fired I felt like my status was tattooed on my forehead in two-inch-high red letters. Although you will proba-

bly feel differently when it happens, remember that termination is not the scarlet letter it once was. In fact, it's a virtual rite of passage. Many people—including perhaps the next person hiring you—have been through it at one time or another. The other thing to remember is that, even in a tight job market, skilled and experienced workers are hard to come by, and that makes you a valuable commodity.

But you do need to decide how you want to discuss it. I recommend against outright lying: the truth has a way of biting back. But there's nothing wrong with "spinning" the story to put it in the best possible light. And these days that should be easy. With so much career mobility and so many reasons for leaving (including "personality clashes," "not seeing eye to eye" with your boss and not "sharing the company's values") you should be able to describe your departure in ways that don't tarnish your reputation or needlessly burn bridges.

If you follow these rules, you should be able to survive being shoved out of the door. At least you'll be a lot better armed than I was the first time I was fired. I was twenty-two at the time and I'd been hired by Big Brothers/Big Sisters to increase the number of volunteers. (The organization pairs at-risk children with adult volunteers to give the kids stable, caring adult attention.) I didn't do anything heroic: I just advertised in the paper and ran a few recruitment seminars. But in my first three months on the job, volunteer applications rose 300 percent. Unfortunately, I "overwhelmed the system," and as a thank-you, I was fired.

And it was lucky I was. A few weeks later I landed a job hosting a public affairs talk show on the radio. It paid a lot better, was a lot of fun and ultimately earned me a journalism award for investigative reporting. But best of all, the radio station gave me the kind of thank-you you can take to the bank.

And you thought being fired was a bad thing!

Working Wounded Poll

If you were suddenly fired what would be the first thing you'd do?

I'd grovel to my boss and pray with all my
   might, 5%
I'd call a lawyer to give them a fight, 25%
I'd just move on and hold no spite, 70%

Poll conducted at *workingwounded.com*

---

from email to *workingwounded.com*

Scrooge Lives!

Last year at the Christmas party, the boss gave us all Christmas cards. We opened them up only to find pink slips inside. He said he thought the party atmosphere would take the edge off of being let go.

The Working Wounded Quotebook

Experience is the name everyone gives their mistakes.

OSCAR WILDE

WHAT TO DO IF YOU THINK YOU'RE GOING TO BE FIRED

Dear WW: *I have a feeling that my boss is about to fire me. In the last few weeks he's been assigning my work to other people and refuses to make eye contact with me. Is there some way I can prepare?*

MY DAYS MAY BE NUMBERED

"I thought it was a myth, but it's true—when you're fired your whole résumé flashes before your eyes."

Dear Numbered,

Axed; canned; discharged; displaced; downsized; dumped; laid off; replaced; riffed; right-sized; sacked; shown the door; asked to resign; terminated . . . If the Inuit have twenty-seven words for snow, what does it mean that we have so many ways to say you're fired?

What it means is that today's workplace is more unpredictable than ever. It means that your company can fire you with *or without* cause (aka the "employment at will" doctrine). If there is a silver lining here, it's that the stigma is gone from being fired because it can happen to anyone at any time. It also means that once you're fired you have a lot more options than you think. The days when you had to take their deal and clear out are gone. Today, unless you've committed a criminal offense, you probably have some room to negotiate with your employer.

Here are strategies that can take some of the charge out of being discharged. They were adapted from the January 15, 1996, issue of *Fortune*.

1. *Keep your cool while the boss delivers the news.* Don't scream, don't sulk. Don't even defend your record. Just listen and take notes. Everything said is potential ammunition for negotiating a termination package. (I recently heard about a case in which the boss said "We really need a man in this position," and the employee cadged a great severance package in exchange for an agreement not to sue for sex discrimination.) By note taking you'll also send the message that you're savvy and not about to surrender.

2. *Know what you need.* Is it:

   a. cash;
   b. good references;
   c. temporary continuation of health care bene-fits;

d. outplacement help; or

e. all of the above?

Look at your bank account, your employability and what you'll need to rebuild your career *before* you start to negotiate a termination package. You probably won't get a blank check from the company, so it's important to focus on what's really important to you.

3. *Get some pros on your side.* A good lawyer is important. But so are other people who have been fired by the company. They've been there. What kind of package did they get? What did they learn in the negotiation process? Learning about others' packages can help you decide what to ask for.

4. *Feed your sense of self-worth.* Two rules I always try to keep: never shop at the supermarket when you're hungry, and never negotiate when you're in the throes of self-doubt. So before you start negotiating, do whatever it takes to renew your self-esteem. Read old compliment letters you've received, call colleagues who you know will say nice things, review past successes. Remember that your firing is probably as much a comment on your boss as it is on you; you needn't feel devalued.

None of this is easy. The company may pressure you to sign their initial offer right away, but you don't have to: you can keep negotiating after you've left the job. Don't wait too long, though, because as your hurt and anger begin to subside, you may find that we missed a word on the list at the top of the column. Rather than "right-sized," "sacked" or "riffed," you may find that you've just been "liberated."

The Working Wounded Quotebook **" "**

If at first you don't succeed, you are running about average.

M. H. ANDERSON

---

from email to *workingwounded.com*

Guess the Knife Cuts Both Ways

One of the weirdest times I've ever had at work was when I was fired. My manager took me into a private room and closed the door. Well, I knew right then what to expect. But before I could get upset, my boss burst into tears. "I've never had to fire someone before," she told me like it was MY problem. So I ended up consoling HER while she was in the process of firing ME!

HOW TO TELL IF THERE IS A LAYOFF
IN YOUR FUTURE

Dear WW: *A friend of mine just got laid off after nineteen years with his company. He says that it came totally out of the blue. I started thinking, could it happen to me? Are there any ways you can tell if your company might be heading toward a layoff?*

CRUISIN' TOWARD A BRUISIN'?

Dear Cruisin',

Your letter reminded me of a conversation I had with a senior executive at a bank while I was running a small start-up. I knew she hated her job so I asked her why she stayed. "For the security," she said. "Your company could disappear tomorrow, but my bank will be here forever." Ten years later my start-up was thriving while her bank was struggling through yet another merger and downsizing. Ironically, the bank changed its name to Security Pacific. But that was the only security she could find—she was laid off shortly after the merger.

If that bank executive had been paying attention to the warning signals, she might have been better prepared. Here's how you can get a general idea of your company's long-range plans . . . and whether you fit into them. Try asking the following questions:

1. *Are sales increasing for your product or service?* Recently Microsoft announced a layoff of people who produce floppy disks because the market is shifting to CDs. The general performance of your company is not as important as the performance of your area. Make friends with co-workers in sales or accounting and see if you can get a peek at sales trends and projections.

2. *How efficient is your company?* Every company has its key efficiency measurements (the retail industry, for instance, measures inventory turns). Find out what measures are important within your department and then contact industry trade associations to find out how your numbers compare to the industry average.

3. *What are your executives really saying?* Learn how to read between the lines of company speeches and publications. Look for warnings about "strong competitors" or moves toward "more efficient operations." ("Efficiency" is often a code word for layoffs.) Look for lengthy explanations about a "difficult environment" (code for declining profits), and beware any move toward off-shore production.

4. *What are the business press and stock analysts saying about your company?* How your company is perceived on Wall Street has an impact on its stock performance. And there's nothing like a falling stock price to persuade executives to take reme-

dial action—most own stock options, after all. Another way to find out what the analysts are saying is to check out *Standard and Poor's* or *Value Line* at your local library.

Conducting an annual "exam" won't prevent you from getting laid off, but it can take the surprise and shock out of the bad news. Even the bank executive from above admitted she should have seen it coming. With a change in the law about where banks can operate, she should have banked on the fact that hers would soon be a takeover target. If she'd been a better business scout, she'd have seen the headlines and could have hit the ground running with her résumé in hand.

The Working Wounded List

When Being Laid Off Isn't So Bad . . . Signs Your Company Might Not Make It

- If the decor is some variation of avocado green and orange, the last time the company could afford to paint was twenty years ago.
- When you ask what systems are in place to protect against viruses and you're sent to the company nurse.

- When there are more vice presidents than there are lead hands on the factory floor.

Economist Nuala Beck via *The Practical Guide to Practically Everything* by Peter Bernstein (Random House, 1996)

The Working Wounded Quiz

If you are laid off your current job and your employer offers you a similar job—and you refuse it—would you still qualify for unemployment insurance?

Answer on page 333.

from email to *workingwounded.com*

They Kissed and *She* Turned into a Frog

I got my first promotion by marrying the assistant manager. I thought I was pretty darn cool until they passed a policy of not being able to work in any section where you were related to the boss. Not only was I demoted, I ended up being let go due to downsizing. That was the quickest trip I ever took up and down the corporate ladder. Next time I'm gonna marry someone lower on the pecking order, so I'll be the one to keep my job.

I WAS FIRED, CAN I FIGHT BACK?

Dear WW: *I've worked for the same company for seven years and was rewarded last week with a pink slip. I asked why, and was told I was an "at will" employee and they didn't need a reason. Can they REALLY do this to me?*
BRUISED AND BATTERED

Dear Bruised,

Remember "Louie Louie"? The song that launched a million frat parties? Well, Richard Berry, the song's lyricist, died recently and in honor of his death we did a little research. Lo and behold, we discovered the following never-released lyric.

Louie, Louie, boss say, "Go!"
Louie, Louie, you say, "No!"
Louie, Louie, you say, "I sue for lotsa dough!"
Louie, Louie, boss say, "Sue and you'll eat crow!"

Who knew Richard Berry would be so pre-scient when it came to employment termination law? You see, there are two types of employees. "Just cause" employees have either a specific employ-ment contract or a collective bargaining agreement that requires their employers to have a "just cause" (in human-talk, "a darn good reason") for dismissal. "At will" employees have no such luck. It's true—your employer *can* fire you with little more than a smile.

Of course, this is a free country—which in the 1990s means you can feel free to sue your employ-er for wrongful termination. But before you do, you should know that such claims are never short, cheap or guaranteed. The successful ones are almost always based on one of the following arguments, so keep them in mind if you decide to proceed:

1. *Were you fired for your race, ethnicity, sex, age, religion, national origin, disability, marital status or (in some places) political affiliation or sexual preference?* Some call it "politically incorrect" but you may be able to call it a lawsuit, because there are numerous laws on the books (including the Americans with Disabilities Act, or ADA, and various civil rights laws) that make it illegal to fire someone for any of these reasons. If you think you've got a case, call the U.S. government's Equal Employment

Opportunity Commission (aka the EEOC) at 800-669-4000.

2. *Were you fired because you refused to do something illegal or because you reported someone who was?* The popular term is "whistleblowing" and numerous laws protect workers from employer retaliation. Talk to a lawyer to check out your rights under both state and federal law.

3. *Were you fired contrary to your personal contract, your union contract or company rules?* If so, you may have a slam-dunk "breach of contract" case—or you may not. Talk to a lawyer to see if the policy violation merits jumping into the ring with your former bosses.

When I talked to Ron Knox, an employment attorney for Seattle-based Garvey, Schubert and Barer, he, of course, followed the lawyers' creed of never dissuading someone from filing a lawsuit. But he also cautioned that employees should think long and hard about the time, money and energy that goes into a drawn-out legal battle. "Remember," he said, "there's no law against your boss being a jerk." To which I said: *Louie, Louie, don't I know!*

The Working Wounded Quotebook

Notice the difference between what happens when a man says to himself, "I have failed three times," and what happens when he says, "I'm a failure."

S. I. HAYAKAWA

The Working Wounded Toolbox

Don't Add Insult to Injury . . . Things Not to Do When You've Been Told You're Fired

- Don't ask for your job back
- Don't debate your performance
- Don't make threats
- Don't immediately agree to negotiate for separation pay
- Don't sign anything

from *Firing Back* by Jodi-Beth Galos and Sandy McIntosh (Wiley, 1997)

from email to *workingwounded.com*

"Janitorial Notification": No Wonder They Call It Cleaning House

The worst thing I've seen in twenty-five years of business was when a co-worker heard about his firing by "janitorial notification." That's what they called it at my company when you discovered you were fired by finding out that they'd changed the lock on your office door. What a way to get paid back for ten years of work.

IN EXCHANGE FOR A SWEETER DEAL, SHOULD I SIGN A NONCOMPETE?

Dear WW: *My department was part of a big company-wide layoff. They offered the standard severance package and then suddenly called me in and offered more money if I signed a noncompete agreement. My friends tell me that I should take the money and not worry, that I can still take a job with a competitor and my current employer will never know. But I'm not sure.*

TO COMPETE OR NOT TO COMPETE

Dear Compete:

Years ago a friend of mine owned a muffin shop in Philadelphia. Martha Stewart had nothing on his muffins. They were huge and mouthwatering-looking, loaded with fruits and nuts. In fact, they were so delicious-looking you were usually two thirds of the way through before you noticed that they tasted like cardboard.

Well, my concern about the sweetened deal your company is offering is that it may look good to you now, but six months down the road may prove just as unpalatable as those muffins. The following questions have been adapted from John Tarrant's *Perks and Parachutes* (Random House, 1997). Give 'em some thought before you make your decision.

1. *Will potential employers be scared off by the noncompete?* Before you trade away your freedom, do some homework. Try to find former employees of your company who signed the agreement and see what luck they've had landing a new job. Also call potential employers and see if they're willing to consider you with the noncompete hanging over your head.

2. *Are you willing to be sued for violating the agreement?* I disagree with your friends who think you can work for a competitor risk-free. The business world can be surprisingly small: your current

employer is likely to hear. And once he's paid you to not compete, he's likely to want to (at least) recoup his money.

3. *If you sign, should you take the money all at once, or spread out the payments?* Many accountants say you should avoid large lump sum payments like the plague. (They can bump you to a higher tax bracket, or worse, you might spend it all at once!) But spreading it out means that your employer maintains control of the cash. And, therefore, you. Personally, I'd consider taking my chances with the IRS and get the cash up front.

4. *Might you regret this decision down the road?* This is one decision that should be made with an eye toward the long term. Unless you've already been planning a career change, you should probably err on the side of freedom.

5. *What did your lawyer say?* It's always a good idea to touch base with an attorney before signing anything. (I know one guy who doesn't even sign birthday cards without legal counsel.)

Before you get cavalier about your employer's offer to throw a few more bucks on the table, remember the words of a friend of mine: "He who has the most lawyers—wins."

The Working Wounded Quotebook

I go where the puck is going to be, not where it is.

WAYNE GRETZKY

from email to *workingwounded.com*

Salt in His Wounds

The worst meeting I ever had was when they told me I'd been laid off but they wanted my input about the company to make it better for FUTURE employees!

The Working Wounded List

Feeling Like You're Running Out of Time? . . . People Who Didn't Make It till After Forty

- Abraham Lincoln
- Harry Truman
- Ray Kroc
- Colonel Sanders

from *Personal Best* by Joe Tye (Wiley, 1997)

"Coles, we've decided to cut back on people named Coles."

HOW HONEST SHOULD I BE ABOUT HAVING BEEN LAID OFF?

Dear WW: *I was laid off and I'm just starting to go out on job interviews again. I'm getting asked a lot about the layoff and I always try to be honest, but I'm beginning to wonder if I'm shooting myself in the foot.*

MONKEY ON MY BACK

Dear Back,

Let me tell you about the best poker player I ever saw. He claimed the world is divided into two kinds of people: poker faces and billboards. With poker faces, you never know what they're thinking. With billboards, one glimpse is all you need to know their whole life's story—and exactly what cards they're holding. He preferred billboards with deep pockets.

Now in the 1990s it's hardly a sin to get laid off (for which we can *thank* AT&T, GM and probably reengineering guru Michael Hammer). But many people still feel shame as well as anger at the company that did the dirty deed. Somehow you've got to get beyond those feelings to survive the interview process. That means you've got to psych yourself up to be a poker face and a billboard at the same time. A poker face when it comes to your bitter or self-reproachful feelings; a billboard when it comes to the facts behind your layoff. Sound impossible? Repeat after me: "I *won't* let my potential employer see that being laid off sucked the life force right outta me. I *won't* let my . . ." And now at the same time: "I'll tell the truth, the whole truth, so help me *L.A. Law.*"

The most important thing to do is show 'em that you've grown. The following questions, adapted from *The Perfect Interview* by John Drake (AMACOM, 1996), should help you come across as both smarter and stronger thanks to your layoff:

1. *Was there anything you could have done to prevent the ax?* Take a look at who got laid off and who

didn't. Do you see a pattern in terms of performance, skills, pay scale, relationships, attitude or tenure? If a pattern emerges, what can you learn from it?

2. *Was there anything your department or company could have done to prevent it?* Was the cutback necessitated by a failure to respond to customers? Competitors? Regulators? By a failure to respond to management's expectations? By a failure to keep costs in line? (I know what you're thinking: "If I knew *that*, Mr. Wounded, I'd have the corner office.") A little 20-20 hindsight may help you understand what happened—*and* impress a potential employer.

3. *What have you learned about yourself from this experience?* Without getting bitter, show your interviewers that you've learned the most important trait in business—the ability to recover from adversity. Avoid upbeat generalities ("I'll always give 110 percent") and instead relate everything you've learned from this experience specifically to the job you're trying to get.

And remember Nietzsche's observation, "That which does not kill, strengthens." To which I'd add, "It'll also help you land another job."

from email to *workingwounded.com*

Eenie Meenie Minie Moe; Let's Use the Computer to Let 'Em Go

At my former company there was a rumor going around that they were going to have a big layoff. I blew it off because my boss had just given me the largest raise that was allowed under our bonus plan, so I figured I was in good shape. Then about a week later I came to work and tried to log onto my computer. The message kept coming back, "invalid entry." That seemed strange so I finally called the folks in the computer department. "Oh yeah," the technician said, "around here that's the way they tell you you've been laid off."

The Working Wounded Quotebook

Failure is success if we learn from it.
MALCOLM FORBES

CHAPTER
11

SICK AND TIRED AND READY TO BE MY OWN BOSS

*Thoughts on Being an
Entrepreneur*

HONEYMOON IN HELL

Are you married to the thought of becoming an entrepreneur? Before you walk down the aisle with your beloved venture, let me tell you a story that illustrates the joys and challenges of entrepreneurship . . .

When I say the word "honeymoon," what pops into your mind? Paris? Maui? Niagara Falls? Those are the places most newlyweds choose. My wife and I, however, did something a bit more revolutionary. But then, I'm probably getting ahead of myself.

When I popped the question (at least a year too

late, according to my wife) we decided that for our honeymoon we wanted to do something out of the ordinary. When the travel agent uttered the magic words "China is cheap," our decision was made. We booked the trip, then turned to all the wedding details—like how to keep a six-foot buffer between the various sets of feuding relatives. (Ah, the joys of family gatherings.)

When the big day finally arrived, I went downstairs to get the newspaper (looking forward to my last long morning constitutional as a bachelor). Imagine my surprise when I saw the headline: *China Declares Martial Law.* It was six weeks into the pro-democracy protests in Tiananmen Square. Now, I'd heard comedians refer to marriage as "going to war," but this seemed to be carrying the metaphor a bit too far.

My wife-to-be and I huddled. Should we go anyway? The trip was planned—heck, it was paid for!—and it would be hard to schedule something else so quickly. Besides, who else had an opportunity to honeymoon under martial law? So, wedding finished, spirits high, we boarded a plane for China.

Our first eight days were intoxicating. We were mobbed by people who, in halting English, wanted to hear about our lives and tell us about their own. As we stood next to the Chinese students' version of the Statue of Liberty in Tiananmen Square, we congratulated ourselves on having made such a brilliant honeymoon choice.

On our ninth day, the massacre occurred in Tiananmen Square.

We left China for Hong Kong, and eventually for the States, and when we got home we called the newspaper to give them a "local angle" on the massacre. They sent a reporter and the following morning we opened the paper to find ourselves on the front page. The headline this time: *Honeymoon in Hell.*

I think of this story—and that headline—every time I think about what it's like to be an entrepreneur. Because what could be more fitting? As an entrepreneur, you experience honeymoon-like bliss at realizing your dream and being your own boss. At the same time you feel like your precarious little venture is going up against the entire Chinese army. It's a paradox.

THE BEST THING ABOUT BEING AN ENTREPRENEUR

In fact, entrepreneuring is one scintillating paradox after another. As one Working Wounded reader pointed out, "The best thing about being an entrepreneur is being your own boss." And, as another

Working Wounded reader pointed out, "The worst thing about being an entrepreneur is being your own boss." It reminds me of an old Vietnam War joke. *What's the difference between the Marines and the Boy Scouts? The Boy Scouts have adult leadership.* And that's the challenge of becoming an entrepreneur. After years of having others call the shots there's suddenly no one but you to play the adult.

If you're already in business for yourself, you already know that. If you're considering becoming an entrepreneur, get prepared. Here are some more paradoxes that will make your sojourn in entrepreneurship seem, at times, like a honeymoon in hell.

THE FIVE PARADOXES OF ENTREPRENEURSHIP

- Paradox No. 1: You need tremendous *people skills* because you're constantly promoting your business, but you've got to survive day to day working largely *on your own.*

  Would-be entrepreneurs think of starting their own business as being set free from the corporate prison, but quickly discover that they've ended up in solitary confinement. Even the co-workers they hated suddenly seem more charming than the silence of their home-based office. The reality is, unless you like your own companionship for eight to twelve hours a day, entrepreneuring's probably not for you. But at the same time, you need to convince potential employees, suppliers and investors that they should be doing business with you. So while you're spending most of your time working alone at your kitchen table, it's your ability to woo and work with others that will spell the success of your venture.

- Paradox No. 2: *You have a sense of urgency* about what you're doing because your paycheck depends on it, but *the people you deal with feel no urgency whatsoever* because they'll get paid regardless.

  For all the hassles of working for someone else, there's wonderful security in collecting a regular paycheck—and that security vanishes when you're out on your own. Instead, every aspect of your business suddenly seems directly related to your ability to bring in cash. Unfortunately the people you work with don't feel that same pressure. While "fast" to you may mean this afternoon, "fast" to someone in a big corporation may mean next Tuesday. So before you poison your relationships by placing undue pressure or unrealistic expectations on employees and suppliers, take a moment to prioritize. Decide if the task at hand is really as urgent as you feel it is. If it is, take the time to explain to the other party *why* it's so important: giving them your insider's perspective may transfer a bit of your urgency as well. If it's not, respect their time line. They'll do a better job for you if they don't sense you're crying wolf.

- Paradox No. 3: You have to be *gentle,* but you have to be *tough.*

  So much of what you do as an entrepreneur is cultivate relationships: with employees, with suppliers, with distributors, with customers, with investors . . . Sometimes it feels as if all you're doing is selling, selling, selling—and the sweet-talking sales mode can get real old. But it's necessary. Without a track record and solid cash flow, you need those relationships to carry you through. At the same time, however, you need to be tough—because if the people you cultivate aren't producing, it's your business that's on the line. That means you need to know when to stop making nice and start turning on the heat.

- Paradox No. 4: You need vision to see the *big picture,* but you also need the ability to sweat the *details.*

  A friend who just started his own consulting business told me a story. He said he'd spent two months preparing a proposal to get work from a local corporation and an additional week prowling to find the best person to give it to. His efforts were rewarded—except for one small detail. The person in question was "Chris" as in "Christopher," not "Chris" as in "Christine." And apparently Chris had taken more than his share of teasing as a kid. He never got past the first line of the proposal and my friend learned the hard way why they say the devil is in the details.

- Paradox No. 5: You spend half your time on *overload* yearning for a day off, and the other half *chewing your nails* wondering when the next customer will show.

    It never rains but it pours. That could be the entrepreneur's motto. You get long fallow periods when you come close to dusting off your résumé to look for a "real job," followed by equally long periods when the work's so thick you can barely come up for air. Tough? You bet. But for most entrepreneurs it's not even a choice. Having tasted freedom, there's no going back. There's one thing you can do when the work is thin, though, besides retype your résumé. Stop worrying and start marketing. That's the only way you'll ever get your nails to grow to their normal length.

These are the paradoxes of entrepreneurship. If you feel you can master them, then go ahead, tie the knot and commit to your new enterprise. Like our honeymoon in hell, it'll be an adventure you'll never forget.

Working Wounded Poll

What is the key to entrepreneurial success?

A cool idea, 27%
Lots of cool cash, 32%
A cool head, 41%

Poll conducted at *workingwounded.com*.

The Working Wounded Quotebook

Remember, this whole thing was started by a mouse.

WALT DISNEY

---

from email to *workingwounded.com*

Home Alone, the Soundtrack

Last year I started a small home-based business. At first the quiet and loneliness made me crazy, but then I found a solution. I bought one of those tapes of office sounds that you can play so customers on the phone will think you're in an office. But I don't use the phone in my business. I just play the tape for myself so I feel like I'm in an office!

DO YOU HAVE WHAT IT TAKES TO BE AN ENTREPRENEUR?

Dear WW: *I'm tired of all of the corporate BS so I'm thinking about going out on my own. But a friend says*

"I'd like to stay, sir, but time is running out if I want to start a rock group."

I'd never make it in business for myself because I don't have the temperament. How can I tell?

GOTTA BE ME

Dear Gotta,

Your letter brings to mind a song that was popular in the 1960s, "Both Sides Now." Feel free to sing along with the Working Wounded updated version:

> *Memos and pulling out your hair, decisions left up*
> *   in the air,*
> *And little tyrants everywhere, I've looked at work*
> *   that way.*
> *But now it only blocks my fun, it makes me mad*
> *   at everyone,*
> *So many things I could have done, but the*
> *   company got in my way!*

I hear from a lot of people who are tired of the corporate BS (it's the number one topic of the letters I receive). And you're not the first to wonder if life wouldn't be better on the outside. For many it is—thousands of intrepid souls have successfully made the transition from tenth-floor cubicle to kitchen table. But your friend is right: it ain't for everyone, and lots more end up selling out the dream than selling stock in their companies.

So let's get right to a series of questions to help you decide if your skills are transferable (also check out Irving Burstiner's book *The Small Business Handbook,* Fireside, 1989).

1. *You're used to playing one role in a big organization. Can you adjust to playing multiple roles in a small shop?* In the corporate world there's a specialist for every detail. In your own shop you're the chief cook and bottle washer. Do you have the skills *and* the patience?

2. *You're used to minimizing risk. Can you learn to love it?* Corporations treat risk the way Japanese chefs treat blowfish: a tiny bit, carefully prepared, and only on special occasions. In start-ups, risk is the main course. Do you have the stomach?

3. *You're used to a steady paycheck. Can you live with less frequent deposits?* Most entrepreneurs start out with Mercedes dreams but keep the Chevy a lot longer than they thought. Are you ready to chuck the expense account for a more humble lifestyle?

4. *You're used to having colleagues. Can you learn to love life on your own?* Your co-workers may drive you crazy, but at least they're there. The support and insight of colleagues is the thing that most entrepreneurs miss the most.

If you've passed this "test"—and if you've got a damn good business idea—go for it! Kiss your boss goodbye. 'Cause as Joni Mitchell never sang:

*Tears and fears and feeling proud, I said, "I'm
    outta here!" right out loud.*
*Dreams and schemes and IPOs, now I look at
    work that way.*
*My old friends are acting strange, they shake their
    heads, they say I've changed,*
*Sure, something's lost, but something's gained:
    I'm working my own way!*

The Working Wounded Quotebook

66 99

***Being on a tightrope is living, everything else
is waiting.***

KARL WALENDA

---

from email to *workingwounded.com*

Now We Know Why the Decision to
Go off on Your Own Is a *Heavy* One

*The hardest thing about working at home is stay-
ing out of the fridge! I've been on my own for six
months now and I've gained nineteen pounds. I'm
thinking about going back to my old job.*

The Working Wounded Quiz

?

Who first coined the word "entrepreneur"?

1. Peter Drucker in the 1970s
2. Tom Peters in the 1980s
3. Steven Covey in the 1990s
4. J. B. Say in the 1800s

Answer on page 334.

THE KEYS TO A SUCCESSFUL BUSINESS PLAN

Dear WW: *I'm part of a start-up and am frustrated by people who seem to think writing a business plan is the most important step we can take. How necessary is one? (We're not borrowing from banks.) And if business plans are so darned important, how come no two people can agree on what's in one?*

> TO PLAN OR NOT TO PLAN,
> THAT IS MY QUESTION

Dear Plan (or am I tipping my hand?),

Years ago I was talking with a mentor about a start-up I was running. He asked to see my business plan and I proudly told him that I didn't have one. Full of youthful arrogance I said, "I'm doing fine just by the seat of my pants." He replied, "If you think you're doing well using your bottom, imagine what you can do using your brain."

So now I'm a born-again planner, but please don't confuse my religious devotion with pleasure. There's nothing I hate more than writing a business plan. It requires weeks of effort, endless trips to the library and tedious analyses of competitors. But it all pays off, because in the words of historian Thomas Carlyle, "Nothing is more terrible than activity without insight," and I know of no better way to get insight about your business than through the discipline of writing a business plan.

Here are the points you want to consider as you start your planning process. They've been adapted from *The Complete Book of Business Plans,* by Joseph Covello and Brian Hazelgren (published by Sourcebooks, 1994).

1. *What is your product or service?* Take off the rose-colored glasses, forget the marketing hype and make an honest comparison with your competition.
2. *Who are your customers?* There are basically two types of customers: virgins (those who currently abstain from your type of product or service)

and those who are married to your competitors. Both are difficult to seduce. As in any wooing situation you've got to know who they are, where they hang out and what turns them on.

3. *What is your strategy for marketing the product or service?* How are you going to reach those "virgins" and "marrieds," and how will you get them to consider your proposal?

4. *How solid are your finances today and what do you project for the future?* This is not the place for dewy optimism. Most businesses fail because they are undercapitalized or because they are unable to manage the money they have.

5. *Does your team have the leadership, skills, and experience to compete?* An honest answer here can save you a lot of pain down the road.

And incidentally, while you're not borrowing from banks right now, I'm willing to bet that won't always be the case, because money to a business is like pigeons to a city dweller. It's not a matter of *if;* it's a matter of *when.* Most people would agree: it's better not to be surprised.

from email to *workingwounded.com*

This Is What You'd Call a Real Nonprofit Operation

When I first went into business for myself, everyone gave me advice. This was the best: "If you sell your products for less than your cost, you will get more customers than the competition because of your low price."

from email to *workingwounded.com*

The Worst Part of Being an Entrepreneur

The worst thing about being an entrepreneur is that if you get in a real jam, you can't say "I was just following orders."

The worst thing about being an entrepreneur is, because of lack of sleep, having to sneak your bed into your office without building security knowing.

The Working Wounded Quotebook   **" "**

The essence of strategy is, with a weaker army, always to have more force at the crucial point than the enemy.

NAPOLEON

SHOULD I INVEST MORE MONEY IN MY BUSINESS?

Dear WW: *I own a small retail business which has been open for two years. We have a great idea, a great location, and business started off well. But for the last year our sales have been going sideways. I'm not sure what the problem is. My manager thinks I need to pump more money into the business to make it grow, but I'm not sure.*

TO SPEND OR NOT TO SPEND

Dear Spend,

My favorite part of the '96 election wasn't Dole's theme song ("Dole Man"). It wasn't the return of Perot's flip charts. It wasn't even the Kemp-Gore face-off. My favorite moment occurred just before Bill and Bob's first debate when the president's staff handed out a press release

311

entitled "Debate Pre-buttal." This deftly named document refuted all the arguments they *expected* Dole to make during the debate. Which just goes to show: Clinton may not be a Boy Scout, but he swears by the oath "Be prepared."

It sounds like you need to do a little "pre-butting" of your own and take a hard look at your business (and substitute your bank loan officer as your "opponent"). Of course, you'll want your review to include all the conventional financial benchmarks (balance sheets, P&L statements and so forth). But also ask yourself the following questions, adapted from James Collins and Jerry Porras's classic *Built to Last* (HarperCollins, 1994):

1. *Are you keeping up with the Joneses?* Remember when banks were only open from 9:00 to 3:00? That was in the old days—before twenty-four-hour supermarkets and an Internet that never sleeps started catering to customers' schedules. Lo and behold: the end of banker's hours. Well, take a look at *your* business and see if you find practices that are equally out of sync with customers' needs. You can't do this from your desk, though. You have to get out and talk with your customers; visit your competitors; and stay in touch with business trends and ideas from other industries.

2. *Do they love me or love me not?* Just how loyal are your customers? Assume not very—and then do

everything you can to woo them. Do customer surveys. Mingle with them on the retail floor. Talk to them when they call. Question them earnestly when they're angry.

3. *Are you ready to take on all comers?* Today ATM machines spit out postage stamps, drugstores push nickel copies, and virtually everything is for sale on the Internet. The days of clear boundaries between businesses are over. What that means for you is you need to guard your back door and keep your eyes peeled for new competitors from unexpected directions.

None of this is easy, of course. It's hard to look at your business through the eyes of a competitor and be critical about your own affairs. But if you can, you'll gain valuable information that will help you decide if throwing money at your business is the proper strategy. Scout's honor.

from email to *workingwounded.com*

Maybe He Should *Invest* in a Punching Bag

The worst thing about being an entrepreneur is that you have to yell at yourself for screwing up 'cause there's no one else to yell at.

The Working Wounded Quotebook

Everything that can be invented has been invented.

CHARLES DUELL,
U.S. Commissioner of Patents, 1899

from email to *workingwounded.com*

Mirror, Mirror on the Wall, Who's the Fairest Boss of All?

The best boss I've ever had (and still have) is myself. Reasons:

1. *I am forgiving (to myself);*
2. *I am generous (to myself);*
3. *I am reasonable (to myself);*
4. *I am approachable (to myself);*
5. *I stand by myself;*
6. *I never give myself a hard time;*
7. *I always support myself;*
8. *I am always fair to myself.*

HOW CAN I GET PEOPLE TO PAY ME ON TIME?

Dear WW: *I run a small business out of my home and suddenly it seems that no one is paying me on time. Help! I need the money.*

SINGING THE COLLECTION BLUES

Dear Singing,

Think about this. It's a beautiful sunny Saturday. Would you rather be:

1. Taking your kid to an amusement park;
2. Scratching around in your garden;
3. Lolling in the hammock with a couple o' cans of beer; or
4. Calling all the people who owe you money?

Let's face it, a root canal is more enjoyable than hounding the deadbeats who owe you money. But to paraphrase the Godfather, Don Corleone (a guy who was seldom stiffed), always keep your friends close and those who owe you money even closer.

It's easier to keep those truants close if you don't lump them all into one group of subhumans, who-don't-really-deserve-the-basic-rights-of-citizenship-like-the-rest-of-us-worthy-types-who-pay-on-time. In *Collection Techniques for the Small Business* (Self-Counsel Press, 1992), Gini Scott and John Harrison suggest that there are lots of reasons for

315

nonpayment and that getting your money often depends on tailoring a strategy to each debtor and the specific reason he's not paying. According to Scott and Harrison, debtors usually fall into one of five categories: *temporarily* unable to pay; able to pay but stalling for some reason that you may be able to negotiate; in dispute with you, in which case there's a whole different issue to resolve; avoiding you for a reason that may be work-out-able; or just plain destitute. Knowing who's in which camp and targeting your strategies accordingly will improve your collection chances.

Here are some questions for you to consider:

1. *Have you talked directly with the people who owe you money?* Face-to-face is best. Letters or conversations with the spouse *don't* count.
2. *Do you know why each one is not paying?* Stop yelling and listen to what they say. You can't have a strategy till you know the reason they're delinquent.
3. *Have you considered all your options?* You can be flexible: drop it, offer a deal or let them pay over time. Or you can be tough: refuse anything but payment in full, repossess, give it to a collection agency or get the pit bulls (oops, I mean lawyers) involved. It may be worth your while to start flexible and then get tougher as the time goes on.
4. *Is it time to reconsider whom you extend credit to?* An

ounce of prevention may be worth a pound of unpaid invoices.

My dad was the master collector of all time. In his car dealership he had his share of debtors from whom he almost always managed to extract his cash. He claimed his secret for success was his tenacity, but after watching him for years I'd say it was something else: his flexibility. For instance, there was the time he accepted golf clubs in exchange for cash he was owed. He played golf all summer and sold the clubs in the fall. Between the golf bets he won and money for the clubs he made more money than the original debt.

So become one with your debtors. Be creative. And don't ever let 'em forget who you are and how much they owe. Not even if it means calling them on a sunny Saturday.

from email to *workingwounded.com*

When the Cash Flow Doesn't

The worst thing about being an entrepreneur can be summed up in five words: baloney sandwiches and bean soup.

The worst thing about being an entrepreneur is being "net 30"!

> The Working Wounded Quotebook
>
> **Great ideas need landing gear as well as wings.**
>
> C. JACKSON

The Working Wounded List

What Were These Entrepreneurs Thinking? . . . Company Names That Just Don't Fly

- Coffin Air Services
- Ransom Air
- Kiwi Air (its namesake, the kiwi bird, doesn't fly)

What's in a Name by Paul Dickson
(Merriam Webster, 1996)

SHOULD I DECLARE MY HOME OFFICE WITH THE IRS?

Dear WW: *I run a business from my home. I want to take a deduction for it, but my accountant tells me home*

"Oh, I love being my own boss, but I hate being my own employee."

offices send a red flag to the IRS. So I'm in the funny position of really working out of my home but not taking the deduction for fear of an audit.

HOME SWEET OFFICE

Dear Home,

A while back, the small business I was running got a call from the IRS. "Just a few questions," they assured me. Next thing I knew we had an IRS agent camped out in our office. And you ain't seen nothin' till you've had the IRS underfoot for a couple weeks. What with all the questions and probing, it was like the Inquisition and a visit to the proctologist rolled into one.

Unfortunately the specter of an audit because of a home office is more real than it used to be—ever since an anesthesiologist named Soliman, who practiced in three hospitals but did his accounting at home, tried to deduct his home office. He argued all the way to the Supreme Court and in 1993 he lost. The Court said his house was not where his money was *earned*. And therefore he couldn't deduct it. So this anesthesiologist effectively put the easy home office deduction to sleep. Now anyone wanting to claim a deduction has to pass three white-knuckling IRS home office "tests." To spare you the Dickensian prose of IRS publication No. 587, "Business Use of Your Home" (masochists can call 1-800-TAX-FORM for their own personal copy), I'll tell you what they are. But take it from me, your accountant has good reason for being conservative.

1. *Where are your dollars earned?* When the IRS talks about your "principal place of business" they aren't talking about where your mail goes or where you do the bookkeeping. They want to know where you earn the money. According to the IRS if most of your work involves meeting clients in their offices, you have no principal place of business—ergo, no place to deduct.

2. *Is the use exclusively for business?* To the IRS life is all work and no play. Any area that you want to deduct at home must be used *only* for business. (The two exceptions are inventory storage and day-care centers). So don't even think about arguing that your new hot tub is exclusively used for entertaining clients.

3. *Is it used regularly?* It takes more than a bowl of prunes to be regular in the eyes of the IRS. They say your home office must be the place where you go predictably and often to do your business.

And speaking of prunes: I want my friends at the IRS to know that I was only kidding about the Inquisition and the proctologists. And that when I made fun of the prose in their publications, it was just a joke. In reality I was moved by No. 587.

from email to *workingwounded.com*

But It Could Probably Come in Useful During an Audit

The worst thing about being an entrepreneur is having to change your voice ten different ways so that potential clients will think you have a good-sized company. At my home-based business I gave myself different names and voices for when I was the secretary, the assistant manager, the appointment manager and the driver. How impressed my future clientele must have been! I guess you can see where this venture ended: belly-up. Although I now have a promising career as a ventriloquist.

The Working Wounded Toolbox

It's My Party (and I'll Cry if I Want to) . . . Who Entrepreneurs Commiserate With

1. *Fellow entrepreneurs, 41%*
2. *Spouse, 23%*
3. *Friends, 13%*
4. *Other, 9%*
5. *No one, 8%*
6. *Other family members, 6%*

Inc. 500 1996 survey of CEOs

The Working Wounded Quotebook

A man's gotta make at least one bet a day, else he could be walking around lucky and never know it.

JIMMIE JONES, horse trainer

CHAPTER 12

DODGING THE BULLETS
How to Find Safety and Meaning at Work

READY FOR A COOL CAREER?

Of all the letters I've received, this one was the toughest to answer: *What advice would you give to someone just starting out?* As I reflected on it I thought about the unexpected twists and turns my own career had taken, and realized that in my entire life I'd met only one person who truly knew what he wanted to do right from the beginning. That person was Marty. At eighteen he had everything all figured out.

I met Marty my senior year in high school when I took a class called Literature for Youth. (We all called it Kiddie Lit.) Other classes in the school reflected a raw, competitive fever, but this one was decidedly more relaxed. Some days you could barely hear Mr. O'Neill over the snoring.

It was while we were discussing *Catcher in the Rye,* I believe, that Mr. O'Neill felt the urge to relate our reading to real life. Unexpectedly he interrupted his discussion of Holden Caulfield and asked the class what we planned to do in the future. One boy nervously volunteered "baseball," two said they wanted to open a garage, four muttered "I dunno." Then Mr. O'Neill came to Marty. "Refrigerator repair," Marty offered as if he'd given the matter a lot of thought. Mr. O'Neill was visibly moved.

"Marty, what a fine career choice. Say it again so everyone can hear. No—wait till I wake up the back row."

It took a few minutes for everyone to shake off their midday slumber but soon all eyes were on Marty. "Refrigeration repair," he said again, and Mr. O'Neill, sensing a chance for peer enlightenment, pressed on. "Marty, tell us how you settled on this particular career."

"My faddah owns da company."

Mr. O'Neill crumpled as if the air had been let out of his tires. Halfheartedly, he resumed the discussion of Holden Caulfield and the back row lowered their heads en masse.

I lost touch with Marty after high school. I imagine he owns the company now (which makes me hope my refrigerator never needs repair). But I bet his path stayed as smooth as his answer that day suggested—no questions about direction or promotion, no struggle to be recognized by the boss, no juggling to conform to illogical company rules.

Unfortunately, most of us are not as lucky as Marty. Our faddahs don't own the company, and we're left to struggle on our own to find the work that's right for us. Once we find it, we're left to dodge the bullets as best we can.

SURVIVING THE SHOOTING GALLERY

Even when the bullets are landing all around you, though, it's possible to remain intact. It just takes pluck and, as Mr. O'Neill used to say, "thick skin and good eyesight." What he meant by that was the ability to disregard life's daily insults while you focus on where you're headed. Now that I'm grown-up, I can see that he was right. In fact, his words are as valuable to someone who's long been in the trenches as they are to someone starting out.

So I borrowed Mr. O'Neill's wisdom when I wrote an answer to that letter. And just in case you've never had a similar pearl passed on to you, I reprint that letter here.

"You're lucky, Dave . . . you've had a heart attack to put your career in perspective."

WHAT ADVICE WOULD YOU GIVE TO SOMEONE JUST STARTING OUT?

Dear WW: *I'm twenty-one and graduating from college in the spring. What business advice would you give to someone just starting out?*

YOUNG AND HUNGRY

Dear Young,

Twenty years ago I asked my mentor, Charlie, the same question. He was CEO of a big company and I thought he was the smartest person I'd ever met. He looked at me with a proud and knowing smile and said, "Bob, the world is divided into sense and nonsense. Your job is to spend your time with things that make sense." For half a second his words rang like an immortal truth. Then I closed my pad and changed the subject. I'd wanted something more than a Hallmark moment.

In the interest of giving you something more than greeting card nonsense, I've adapted some points from an insightful book called *We Are All Self-Employed,* by Cliff Hakim (Berrett-Koehler, 1994). Hakim's main point is that if you want to be gratified by work, you need to proactively manage your career: you need to decide your next steps, acquire the necessary skills and actively pursue your choices. Your employers won't do this for you. As a friend once observed, "It's a corporation you work for—not your mother."

Along the way these tips may help:

1. *Expect discomfort.* As Scott Peck noted in *The Road Less Traveled,* "Life is difficult." Well, so is work!—even a job you love. The lucky workers are the ones who can see past the irritations and remember (as they say about marriage) why they fell in love in the first place.
2. *Keep learning.* The years I learned the *least* were the years I spent getting my MBA. On the other

hand, this last year I learned how to design a Web site, how to do TV stand-ups and how to sail. The best way to keep your career in shape is to keep your learning muscles buffed. My strategies: read a book every month that will give you new skills or insight, and hang out with smart people who really love what they do.

3. *Love the one you're with.* Some folks are incredibly lucky: they can make a career out of something they already love. For most of us, though, the challenge is a little tougher. We need to find a way to love the thing we're doing. Remarkably, that isn't so hard. Instead of just taking the jobs that companies hand you, *stretch* your jobs, make them your own. Instead of just fulfilling each job's requirements, turn the job into something that fulfills you. When you've eked out all the growth and learning, move on.

Recently I asked a venture capitalist the most important thing he looks for when investing in a business. His reply? "Passion." It's no different for you. *Find the passion in every job, don't let discomfort extinguish it, and stoke your passion with learning.* You'll be making a sound investment in your career. I hope this makes *sense!*

KEEPING YOUR CAREER OUT OF THE DEEP FREEZE

There's a follow-up to the Marty story. Some years ago, my refrigerator *did* break and I called a refrigerator repairman. He explained that the reason it wasn't getting cold was because the freezer was filled with ice. "How can that be?" I asked. "It's a frost-free refrigerator." The guy looked at me with an expression that reminded me of my Uncle Herm when he was about to impart some Old Country wisdom. "Son," he said, "there ain't no such thing as a frost-free refrigerator." Then, on an invoice that bore the slogan "America's Best Frost-Free Refrigerator," he wrote out my bill.

And that about sums up my thoughts on the workplace: it gives you more frost than you need—and gives it when you least expect it—but you depend on it for your supper.

So how do you cope? You get out the Working Wounded toolbox and try to repair the damage.

"Intrapreneuring, chief—how about a glass on the house?"

MANKOFF

The Working Wounded Quotebook

"" ""

Don't fight forces. Use them.

BUCKMINSTER FULLER

---

from email to *workingwounded.com*

What to Do When All Else Fails

Imagine them naked.

WORKING WOUNDED
QUIZ ANSWERS

CHAPTER 2

Two employees with the same job title can be paid different amounts. It's what they do that matters.

"Job titles aren't decisive in assessing whether two jobs are equal; it's the work duties that count." Fred Steingold, *The Employer's Legal Handbook* (Nolo Press, 1997, page 3/15).

CHAPTER 3

Student loans can be garnished by an employer. The other items in the quiz are considered "sacrosanct."

"The U.S. Department of Education . . . may garnish up to 10% of a former student's net pay . . . [The rest is] considered sacrosanct and may not usually be deducted from an employee's paycheck." Barbara Repa, *Your Rights in the Workplace* (Nolo Press, 1996, page 3/61, 3/63, and 3/64).

CHAPTER 4

Not unless you want to open yourself to a lawsuit. You should tell prospective employers only what you can prove to be true. Poor performance on the job is relatively easy to prove. A drinking problem probably would be much harder to prove.

"To win a defamation case, a former employee must prove that you gave out false information and that the information harmed his or her reputation. If you can prove the information you gave out was true, the defamation case will be dismissed." Fred Steingold, *The Employer's Legal Handbook* (Nolo Press, 1997, page 10/41).

CHAPTER 5

None. Under no conditions can your employer force you to stay in your job.

"The other side of the employment at will logic is that employees are also free to leave a job at any time; an employer cannot force you to stay in a job you no longer wish to keep." Barbara Repa, *Your Rights in the Workplace* (Nolo Press, 1996, page 10/4).

CHAPTER 6

False. Verbal statements have been considered legally binding by the courts.

"Statements you make during interviews and when making job offers may later be treated as binding contracts. Fred Steingold, *The Employer's Legal Handbook* (Nolo Press, 1997, page 1/9).

CHAPTER 7

Yes. Your employer would have to pay you at least the minimum wage as long as you spent more than 20 percent of your time selling and you work at the employer's place of business. In all cases, however, an employee's pay divided by the hours worked during the pay period must equal or exceed the minimum wage (Under the Fair Labor Standards Act). Barbara Repa, *Your Rights in the Workplace* (Nolo Press, 1996, page 3/9).

CHAPTER 8

You lose your job and your employer has only fifteen employees. Your employer is required to offer insurance for any sin short of "gross misconduct." "COBRA, requires . . . continuing insurance coverage if: you lose insurance coverage because your number of work hours is reduced, or you lose your job for any reason other than gross misconduct. . . . (applies to all employers with 20 or more employees). Under the law, employers need only make the insurance available; they need not pay for it." Barbara Repa, *Your Rights in the Workplace* (Nolo Press, 1997, page 4/5).

CHAPTER 9

No. Your employer cannot listen to your personal phone calls. A personal call can only be monitored with your permission.

"If a call is being monitored for business reasons, which is perfectly legal, if a personal call comes in, an employer must hang up as soon as he or she realizes that the call is personal. An employer may monitor a personal call only if an employee knows the particular call is being monitored." Barbara Repa, *Your Rights in the Workplace* (Nolo Press, 1996, page 6/41).

CHAPTER 10

No. You would probably be disqualified from receiving unemployment insurance with a legit job offer.

"Even if you are covered by unemployment insurance and otherwise eligible to receive it, you may be disqualified . . . if you refused to accept a similar job without good reason." Barbara Repa, *Your Rights in the Workplace* (Nolo Press, 1996, page 12/3).

CHAPTER 11

4.   J. B. Say in the 1800s.

"'The entrepreneur,' said the French economist J. B. Say around 1800, 'shifts economic resources out of an area of lower and into an area of higher productivity and greater yield.'" Peter Drucker, *Innovation and Entrepreneurship* (Harper & Row, 1983, page 21).

ACKNOWLEDGMENTS

Ever watch the Academy Awards when some obscure winner drones on and on thanking the *really* little people (" . . . and thanks to the people who washed my costumes . . .")? Good, because I think you already have a sense of what's to follow. Don't say I didn't warn you!

First and foremost, I'd like to thank all of the readers and viewers of Working Wounded. Without your email and letters, problems and strategies, compliments and criticism this book wouldn't have been possible. Thanks to Scott Adams who proved that you *can* sell books to people in the shallow end of the corporate pool and Robert Mankoff for contributing so many wonderful cartoons to this book.

After hearing the complaints of many other writers, I have no doubt that Mel Parker is the best editor, publisher and co-conspirator a writer could ever have. The enthusiasm and commitment that he's mobilized for this unheard-of author is, well, unheard of. (My only regret is that I wasn't on the phone when the Working Wounded version of *Both Sides Now* was sung to *Publishers Weekly.*) Mel, thanks for being such a mensch. I'd also like to thank all the other members of the Warner family who helped make this book possible (Sharon, Harvey-Jane, Thom, Flag, and Ann).

There is an old saying, behind every "hack" columnist is a really excellent writer. And *Working Wounded* is no exception. As the most talented writer in our home, my wife, Robin, contributed her wit and wisdom from the first proposal to the final draft. And for all those nights she gave up writing her beloved fiction for *Working Wounded,* I'm eternally grateful. Speaking of writing talent in our home—I also must thank our daughter, Hallie, the second most accomplished writer at our house and a never-ending source for *Working Wounded* stories.

My only sorrow is that my mother and father died before this book was published. A special thanks to Kay, who gave me my sense of humor, and Henry, who gave me my nose for business. In so many ways, the blend of humor and information in *Working Wounded* is a tribute to both of you.

Also thanks to Jay and Deena and the rest of my extended family for allowing me to reveal so many of our family stories and secrets. And speaking of extended family, a big thanks to Jim for being my comedy inspiration and the greatest manager that the BHS Tennis Team ever had. And Mark, who's been a friend since our mothers put us in the crib together as infants (and we've been peeing and pooping on each other ever since). I also thank all my friends in Lincoln Park, Boonton High, Seattle and on Bainbridge Island, who've tolerated me through a very protracted childhood.

I feel blessed to be represented by James Levine Communications (Jim, Daniel, Melissa and Ariel) who, thankfully for this novice author, do not view their job as being over when a book is sold. Thanks for being there for me at every step of the process from advising me on how to write the proposal to providing a crash pad during visits to NYC (And to anyone still reading this who is a friend of Daniel—ask him to tell you the Dennis Rodman story).

Next in line are the newspapers that gave Working Wounded its start. I'm forever in debt to *Eastsideweek*'s

ACKNOWLEDGMENTS

Knute, Helen and David for believing in my crazy idea for a weekly column. Also special thanks for Cathy and Jacky at the *News Tribune* (Tacoma, WA), Kevin at the *Sun* (Bremerton, WA) and Sherry at the *News & Observer* (Raleigh, NC) for being the first members of the Working Wounded dysfunctional family. All of you need to realize that I don't hold hands with just anyone. Also thanks to all of the other Working Wounded papers: *New York Daily News, San Francisco Examiner, Oregonian, Seattle Times, Wilmington News Journal, Sacramento Gazette, Inland Valley Daily Bulletin, San Bernardino Sun, Gainesville Sun, Idaho Statesman, Arlington Heights Daily Herald, Owensboro Messenger & Inquirer, St. Paul Pioneer Press, Billings Gazette, Albuquerque Tribune, Albany Times Union, Amarillo Daily News/ Globe, Deseret News, Walla Wall Union-Bulletin* and *Yakima Herald Republic.*

Another early believer in Working Wounded is Dave, the czar of Costco Online and the Costco Connection. Thanks for being there right from the start and for giving me the honor of talking every month to the Costco extended family. (Thanks too to Anita, Pam, Lani, Jace, Bob, Todd, Tony, Angie, everybody involved with the Connection and Costco Online.)

Thanks to Cyndi at the *Seattle Times* for introducing me to John, Robert and the entire United Media crew (Rebecca, Suma, Lisa, Liz, Mary Anne, Peter, etc.) and to the remarkably talented Matt and Brian.

Oh, no. He's not done yet.

The "new and improved" workingwounded.com wouldn't have been possible without the help of Jeff, Ian, Gif, Libba, Torino and Michele.

And thanks to all of the people I've worked with through the years because they all taught me lessons (or

Acknowledgments

gave me stories) that I drew on for *Working Wounded*. From my first jobs as a car jockey at Lincoln Park Motors and teaching tennis at Boonton High School, to later gigs at American University, Jay Rosner for Congress Campaign, the Eatery, University of Puget Sound Student Programs, Western State Hospital, Big Brothers, KNBQ, Safety Assistance from the Elderly, Group Health Cooperative, Seattle University, Smoking Policy Institute, E.P.A., Seattle Pacific University, King County Medical, United Way of King County, Solveris, Mainstream Online, Science Club, NetStockDirect, the Seattle Public Schools, KOMO, and of course, workingwounded.com. (Do you get the sense that I have trouble holding a job?) Also let me list a few of the rich volunteer opportunities that have taught me so much: Lions Club of Lincoln Park, Peoples Bi-Centennial Commission, Congresswoman Bella Abzug, Food Bag Coop, Rotary Club of Seattle, United Way, Guardian Ad Litem, the Salvation Army and the Giraffe Project.

Thanks to Shaun Hubbard, who designed the Working Wounded logo. And finally, a special thanks to Joanna Cannon Lupy, who gave the greatest gift of all.

Let me sum up how I feel right now by quoting Kermit the Frog during his commencement address at Long Island University in 1996. "All of us should feel very proud of ourselves, and just a little bit silly."

And thanks to Serni for taking the Working Wounded lecture series on the road. Also thanks to Dan, Anne, Jon, Jim and Kathy.

BOB, Chairman & Shop Steward
July 1997